THE COMMERCIAL RESTRAINTS
OF IRELAND

LECTOR HOUSE PUBLIC DOMAIN WORKS

THE COMMERCIAL RESTRAINTS OF IRELAND

JOHN HELY HUTCHINSON,
W. G. CARROLL

ISBN: 978-93-5614-459-0

Published: 1882

LECTOR HOUSE LLP
E-MAIL: lectorpublishing@gmail.com

From a painting by Sir Joshua Reynolds.

THE COMMERCIAL RESTRAINTS OF IRELAND

CONSIDERED IN A SERIES OF LETTERS TO A NOBLE LORD, CONTAINING AN HISTORICAL ACCOUNT OF THE AFFAIRS OF THAT KINGDOM. DUBLIN, 1779.

BY

JOHN HELY HUTCHINSON,

PROVOST OF TRINITY COLLEGE, ETC.

"— —the best exposition which exists of the poisonous forces which had so long been working in the country." —*Froude.*

"This valuable and rare book is, perhaps, the best ever written on the subject of Irish trade, and the restrictions put upon it by England." —*Mr. Blackburne.*

RE-EDITED, WITH A SKETCH OF THE AUTHOR'S LIFE, INTRODUCTION, NOTES, AND INDEX, BY W. G. CARROLL, M.A.

S.S. BRIDE'S AND MICHAEL LE POLE'S, DUBLIN.

"Good Heaven! for what peculiar crimes,
Beyond the guilt of former times,
Is Ireland ever doom'd by fate
To groan beneath Oppression's weight." —*Baratariana.*

"If your vessel is frequently in danger of foundering in the midst of a calm, if by the smallest addition of sail she is near over-setting, let the gale be ever so steady, you would neither reproach the crew nor accuse the pilot or the master; you would look to the construction of the vessel and see how she had been originally framed and whether any new works had been added to her that retard or endanger her course." —*Commercial Restraints.*

The Publishers desire to express their best thanks to the Provost and Senior Fellows of Trinity College for their kindness in lending the Library copy of the "Commercial Restraints," and the portrait of Provost Hely Hutchinson, by Sir Joshua Reynolds; also for the extracts from the College Register, and for free access to the Matriculation and Judgment Books.

The Publishers have, likewise, to acknowledge their obligation to Sir Samuel Ferguson for the courteous favour of the fac-simile of Provost Hutchinson's autograph which underlines the frontispiece.

CONTENTS

LIFE OF PROVOST HELY HUTCHINSON.

THE RIGHT HON. JOHN HELY HUTCHINSON, author of the "Commercial Restraints," was certainly one of the most remarkable men that this country ever produced; and he took, amidst an unequalled combination of brilliant rivals, a very prominent part in the most interesting and splendid period of Ireland's internal history. He was, according to Dr. Duigenan, a man of humble parents. He entered Trinity College as a Pensioner, in the year 1740, under the name John Hely,[1] and after his marriage he adopted the name Hutchinson, on succeeding to the estate of his wife's uncle.

In 1744 he obtained his B.A., and Duigenan admits that in his Undergraduate Course he won some premiums at the quarterly examinations. In 1765 he was presented with the degree of LL.D. *Honoris Causâ*. The *College Calendar*, in the list of Provosts, has, "1774. The Rt. Hon. John Hely Hutchinson, LL.D., educated in Trin. Coll., Dublin, but not a Fellow; admitted Provost by Letters Patent of George III., July 15; Member of Parliament for the City of Cork, and Secretary of State. Died Provost, Sep. 4, 1794, at Buxton."[2]

This is all the mention which the published records of the College make of, perhaps, its most celebrated Provost. The Calendar is inaccurate as to the year of his matriculation, and it does not even tell that he was the author of the "Commercial Restraints"—its memorial notices being extremely scanty and brief; but in other contemporary writings we find several notices of him, unfavourable and favourable. He was called to the Bar in 1748; King's Counsel, 1758; Member for Lanesborough as John Hely Hutchinson of Knocklofty, 1759;[3] in 1760 he received, in a silver case, the freedom of Dublin for his patriotic services in parliament.[4] He was Member for Cork City as John Hely Hutchinson of Palmerston, and afterwards as Right Hon., 1761; Prime Serjeant, sometimes going Judge of Assize, and

---

[1] His Matriculation is—"1740, April 29th. Johannes Hely, Filius Francisci Gen. Annum agens 17. Natus Corcagii. Educatus sub Dr. Baly. (Tutor) Mr. Lawson."

[2] See Note A.

[3] Hutchinson had thus achieved very considerable success and distinction when he was thirty-seven years of age—"the fatal year" in the development of genius, according to Lord Beaconsfield. Grattan accomplished his great work at the age of thirty-six, the age at which Lord Byron had finished his poetry. Fitzgibbon, too, ran high in this respect. At twenty-nine he was a leading lawyer, and M.P. for the University, having displaced and replaced the Provost's son; at thirty-four he was Attorney-General, governing the country. He was Lord Chancellor and a peer before he had attained what Dr. Webb, in his "Faust," calls "the mature age of forty-one." He died at 53.

[4] [Pue's Occur.]

Privy Councillor, 1761; Alnager,[5] 1763; Major in a Cavalry Regiment, which, when threatened with a court-martial for non-attendance to duty, he sold forthwith for £3,000; Provost and Searcher of Strangford,[6] 1774; Principal Secretary of State, 1777;[7] M.P. for Taghmon, 1790; died 1794 (according to the *College Calendar* at Buxton, and according to the *Gentleman's Magazine* in Dublin). He was also Treasurer of Erasmus Smith's Board, and one of the Commissioners for inquiring into Education Endowments, and he strove perseveringly but fruitlessly to obtain besides the Chancellorship of the Exchequer.

The most important and most historic of all these appointments was the Provostship, and it is in connection with the Provostship that we know most about him. He won the high office, for which, in regard of any sort of learning, he was totally disqualified, by a dexterous intrigue with the Chief Secretary of the day, Sir John Blacquiere; and those who cared most for Hutchinson considered that the manœuvre was an unwise one for him. It forfeited his assured prospects at the Bar, and it fastened on him the odious imputation of an insatiable avarice. The appointment, moreover, was regarded as an affront and an injury by the body over which he was placed. Fellows and Scholars in various ways resented the indignity, and Hutchinson had to face a very surly temper inside the walls. He faced it with a light heart, and triumphed over it; but it often turned on him, and stung him. He considered that it was well worth the cost; for in the first place it was an appointment for life; and then he had not to give up his lucrative practice in the law courts, which Froude says was worth nearly £5,000 a year; and in fact he never ceased to angle for the Mastership of the Rolls. In the next place, he got in addition a splendid town residence, on which eleven thousand pounds had just been expended; he got an income of two thousand one hundred a year; he got a very wide patronage, and he calculated on getting the control of the parliamentary representation of the University, which at that time was in the hands of the Fellows and Scholars. This last object would have been an immense acquisition for him; but he failed to win the game, the playing of which led him, according to Duigenan and others, into some of his most reprehensible courses.

As has been said above, in the rivalries of public life Hutchinson was pitted against a phalanx of as able men as ever appeared together in any country; and most of these men he supplanted and surpassed. They avenged themselves by lampooning him, and they were masters in the art. The Provost was assailed in prose and in verse, in couplet and in cartoon, in newspapers and pamphlets, in the "Lachrymæ Academicæ," "Baratariana," and "Pranceriana;" and these two last *pasquinades* are unique in English literature. Their satire is as broad and as wounding as that of Junius, while it is often far more finished and playful; and there is no other instance of so many men of the same ability and station being combined in such a mosaic of detraction.[8]

[5] Alnager, or Aulnager, from the Latin *Ulna*, an ell, was an officer for measuring and stamping cloth in the wool trade. *Pranceriana Poetica* has the line:—

 "Send Prancer back to stamping friezes."

[6] See his will.

[7] See Note E.

[8] Lord Lieutenant Townshend's organ was "The Batchelor; or, Speculations of Jeof-

"BARATARIANA," so called from Sancho Panza's island-kingdom, was written in verse and in prose, and it appeared originally as letters in the *Freeman's Journal*, which at that time, previous to its removal to "Macænas' Head" in Bride-street, was published over St. Audeon's Arch.[9] The principal writers of these letters were Sir Hercules Langrishe,[10] Flood, Grattan, Yelverton, Gervase Bushe, and Philip Tisdall. The volume is "a collection of pieces published during the administration of Lord Townshend," and in it the Lord Lieutenant figures as "Sancho," Anthony Malone as "Don Antonio," Provost Andrews as "Don Francesco Andrea del Bumperoso," and Hely Hutchinson under the various titles of "Don John Alnagero, Autochthon, Terræ Filius, Monopolist, Single Session, and Serjeant Rufinus." It was in one of these papers that Grattan, with an audacious drollery, drew his celebrated character of Lord Chatham, as a privileged extract from a manuscript copy of Robertson's forthcoming "History of America." The description given by Langrishe of Hutchinson, who was not Provost at that time, is: "He talks plausibly and with full confidence, and whatever Pro-consul is deputed here Rufin immediately kidnaps him into a guardianship, and like another Trinculo erects himself into a viceroy over him. His whole elocution is alike futile and superficial. It has verdure without soil, like the fields imagined in a Calenture. He has great fluency, but little or no argument. He has some fancy, too, but it serves just to wrap him into the clouds and leave him there, while he holds himself suspended, planing and warbling like a lark, without one thought to interrupt the song. If he has any forte it is in vituperation or abuse. In 1766 he defeated the first Militia Bill.[11] His first stride in apostasy was supporting the Privy Council Money Bill in 1767 [for opposing which Anthony Malone[12] had previously lost the Prime Serjeancy in 1754, and the Chancellorship of the Exchequer[13] in 1761;] his next was in defending the motion for the additional regiments, whereby we were treated like a ravaged country, where contributions are levied to maintain the very force that oppresses it." For these ministerial services Hutchinson got the Prime Serjeancy, with an extra salary of £500 a year. In the next session he was useful to the Crown in regard of the Penfrey Wagstaffe, Esq.," published at the *Mercury* in Parliament-street, by one Hoey, a popish printer. To be "mimicked by Jephson and libelled by Hoey," were amongst the social terrors of the period. —[*Baratariana*.]

[9] *Pranceriana* has the line, "To storm her fane in Owen's Arch."

[10] It was Sir Hercules Langrishe who accounted to Lord Lieutenant Townshend for the marshy and undrained condition of Phœnix Park, by observing that the English Government "had been too much engaged in *draining* the rest of the kingdom."

[11] In 1779 the arms which had been intended for the Militia were given by Government to the Volunteers, the Militia Enrolment Act of the previous years not having been carried out, from want of money.

In 1783 the Volunteers were—prematurely—disbanded, and in 1785 the Militia were enrolled, and Langrishe's Bill obtained from parliament £20,000 for clothing them. Subsequently the Commissioners of Array were appointed.

[12] Anthony Malone, along with so many other grandees of the period, lived in Chancery-lane. It requires an effort of historic faith to realise that the Chancery-lane of to-day was a couple of generations ago the abode of such fashion and rank. The fact, however, is quite certain. St. Bride's Vestry Book contains a copy of Anthony Malone's and Alexander MacAulay's Opinions *in re* Powell's Legacy to the Dublin parishes.

[13] See note E.

sions Enquiry Bill and the Embargo Corn Bill, and was rewarded with the sinecure Alnager's place, worth £1,000 a year. He was made a Privy Councillor, got the reversionary grant of the Principal Secretaryship of State, and the commission of a half-pay majority, and was what Primate Stone termed "a ready-money voter." "He got more," says Flood, "for ruining one kingdom than Admiral Hawke got for saving three."[14] The "List of the Pack," one of the rhymes in the volume, has:

> "Yet Tisdal unfeeling and void of remorse,
> Is still not the worst—Hely Hutchinson's worse;
> Who feels every crime, yet his feeling denies,
> And each day stabs his country, with tears in his eyes."

Philip Tisdall, in "Baratariana," gives the following humorous description of Hutchinson: "He is jealous of me, and as peevish as an old maid. I love to tease him. I endeavour to put him on as odious ground as I can in parliament, and then I am the first to complain to him that Government should expose their servants to so much obloquy without occasion. I magnify to him the favours and confidence I receive from Government, and my correspondence with Rigby, which nettles him to the heart. He is too finical for Lord Townshend, who makes very good sport of him. One day he dined at the Castle, and when the company broke up, Lord Townshend, who pretended to be more in liquor than he was, threw his arms about his neck and cried out, 'My dear Tisdall, my sheet anchor, my whole dependence! don't let little Hutchinson come near me; keep him off, my dear friend; keep him off—he's damned tiresome.' At other times His Excellency makes formal appointments to dine at Palmerston[15] at a distant day. The Prime Serjeant invites all the officers of State; Mrs. Hutchinson is in a flurry; they send to me for my cook; and after a fortnight's bustle, when dinner is half spoiled, His Excellency sends an excuse, and dines with any common acquaintance that he happens to meet in strolling about the streets that morning. This g'emman has a pretty method enough of expressing himself, indeed, but in points of law there are better opinions. My friend, the late Primate, who knew men, said, that the Prime Serjeant was the only person he had ever met with who got ready money, in effect, for every vote he gave in parliament. He has got among the rest the reversion of my Secretary's office; but I think I shall outlive him."[16]

Another note in "Baratariana" records that Tisdall, whose Government salaries exceeded £5,000 a year, had also a reversion of the Alnager's place, with its £1,000 a year, on the death of Hutchinson; and this mutuality of Reversions, no

---

[14] Froude details the bargain. In 1771 it was important to secure for the Army Augmentation Bill the support of Hutchinson, who had been patriotising on the Surplus, Pension, and Septennial Bills. His terms to Lord Lieutenant Townshend were, "a provision for the lives of his two sons, one aged 11 and the other 10, by a grant to them or the survivor of them of some office of at least £500 a year. If no vacancy occurred, then either a pension, or a salary to that amount to be attached to some office for them—and his wife to be created a Viscountess."—"English in Ireland," vol. i., p. 632, and elsewhere.

[15] Palmerston, the Provost's private country residence, was a noble and beautifully situated mansion on the banks of the Liffey, between Chapelizod and Lucan. It is now occupied by Stewart's Idiot Asylum.

[16] Tisdall did not outlive him, and Hutchinson got the Principal Secretaryship.

doubt, accounts for the warm affection that subsisted between Hutchinson and Tisdall. Blacquiere got the Alnagership as the price of the Provostship, as before mentioned. Besides the Alnagership Hutchinson was obliged also to resign the Prime Serjeancy, which was given to Dennis; but even in regard of emolument the Provostship was well worth these two sacrifices, the united income of which was only £1,300. He retained his sinecure of £1,800 a year, and the State Secretaryship, and he was further compensated by the sinecure office of Searcher of the Port of Strangford, with a patented salary of £1,000 a year for his own life and the lives of his two elder sons. He had thus altogether, besides his lucrative practice at the Bar and his own estate, about £6,000 a year, together with the Provost's House, while his eldest son was Commissioner of Accounts, with £500 a year, and with the reversion of the Second Remembrancership of the Exchequer, worth £800 a year, and his second son had a troop of dragoons.[17]

"Pranceriana" derives its title from "Prancer," or "Jack Prance," the nickname which was given to the Provost,

> "Restorer of the art of dancing,
> And mighty prototype of prancing,"

from his effort to establish in the College a riding and dancing-school, in imitation of the Oxford schools.

> "Each college duty shall be done in dance,
> And hopeful students shall not walk, but prance."

The articles were originally published in the *Hibernian Journal* and *Freeman's Journal*,[18] and the two volumes, which appeared in 1776, were announced as "A collection of fugitive pieces published since the appointment of the present Provost." The collection was dedicated to "J-n H-y H-n, Doctor of Laws, P.T.C., late Major in the Fourth Regiment of Horse, Representative in the late and present Parliament of the city of Cork, one of his Majesty's Counsel at Law, Reversionary Remembrancer of the Exchequer, Secretary of State, one of His Majesty's Most Honourable Privy Council, and Searcher, Packer, and Gauger of the Port of Strangford."[19]

[17] One of the severest letters in the collection is No. 22, on Edmund Sexten Pery, who, for fourteen years, was Speaker of the House of Commons. Patriotic and eminent as Pery was, and upright and loyal as he always was in the Chair, it cannot be denied that he got the Speakership by an unworthy manœuvre. The passage is fully and bitterly rehearsed in the last volume of the Historical Manuscript Reports. Pery was bought by the corrupter Townshend at the same time with Hutchinson, Tisdall, Flood, &c.

[18] The Court of King's Bench granted an information in the name of the king, at the prosecution of the Right Hon. Hely Hutchinson, against Samuel Leathley, the printer of the *Freeman's Journal*, for publishing in that paper the article signed "Crito," in November, 1776. The article is not in the "Pranceriana." — [*Freeman's Journal*, June 9th, 1777.]

[19] The *Pranceriana Poetica*, or *Prancer's Garland*, published in 1779, opens,

> "A harlequin provost, cognomine prancer;
> A duellist, scribbler, a fop, and a dancer;
> A lawyer, prime sergeant, and judge of assizes;
> A parliament man, and a stamper of friezes;
> A councillor privy; a cavalry major;
> A searcher and packer, comptroller and gauger;

It attacks the Provost all round with every asperity; it mocks his want of learning by calling him "the Potosi of Erudition;" it makes fun of his riding and dancing-schools; and it ridicules his boasted college reforms.

Alluding to his efforts to banish card-playing there is the rhyme—

> "You bag and baggage made them pack
> Old Whist, and Slam that Saucy jack,
> Ombre, Quadrille, Pope Joan, Piquet,
> And Brag and Cribbage—cursed set."

It is obliged to admit, however ungraciously, that the Provost effected some improvements. He obtained from the Erasmus Smith board, of which he was treasurer, the £200 a year for the oratory and composition premiums,[20] as well as the £2,500 for building the theatre, which Duigenan declares the College did not want. He established also the Modern Languages Professorships, the latter-day English Parliament treatment of which is such a curious passage in the history of the University. "Pranceriana" admits, too, that by the Provost the park was walled in,[21] and that common rooms inside the walls, supplied with coffee and papers, were provided for the students; that "tardies" [i.e. returns of students as passing

---

> A speecher, a critic, prescriber of rules;
> A founder of fencing and 'questrian schools.
> If various employments can give a man knowledge,
> Then who knows so much as the head of the College?
> *   *   *   *   *
>
> The Seniors and Juniors in this are agreed,
> As a Consul of Rome was Caligula's steed;
> They very much fear that if Prancer was dead
> Sir John would appoint a Jackass in his stead."

(Halliday Collection)

This book also is a collection of fugitive pieces, and it is dedicated to "Sir John Blacquiere, Knight of the Bath, Alnager of all Ireland, and Bailiff of the Phœnix Park." There is not a copy in the College Library. The Royal Irish Academy copies have the excellent woodcuts. In an autograph note to his own copy of the book, Dr. Stock, F.T.C.D., afterwards Bishop of Killala, says that the engravings were made by his brother, Mr. Frederick Stock, who kept a woollen draper's shop in Dame-street. He states that the printer, Michael Mills, was forced from his house by a party of college lads, who conveyed him to the College, and there pumped on him; and that the late Prime Serjeant Browne, then a student, had a share in the outrage. Dr. Stock gives the key to the "Poetica," viz.—Moderator, Prancer, and Hipparchus = the Provost; Dr. Pomposo and Mendex = Dr. Leland; Matthew Ben Sadi and Dr. Dilemma = Dr. Forsayeth; Billy Bib = Dr. Hales; and Bezabel Black-letter = Michael Mills. A copy of the extract is in the possession of Mr. Traynor, Bookseller, Essex-quay.

[20] "Pranceriana Pœtica" says that the Provost multiplied the composition premiums as means of bribery. It gives one of the Provost's advertisements (1777): "Any student may be a candidate for all, or for *any more* of the said premiums!"

[21] In Sir Bernard de Gomme's map of the city and harbour of Dublin, in 1673, given in Mr. Prendergast's edition of "The Scandinavian Kingdom of Dublin," p. 229, the college park is marked as set out in paddocks. Dr. Stubbs says that the park was thrown into its present champaign form, laid out, and planted in the year 1722, as appears from "Winstanley's Poems," vol. i., p. 269. Dublin: 1742.

into College between 9 and 12 P.M.] were lessened, that "chapels" required to be attended by them were increased, and that the calling of examination rolls was finished by eight o'clock in the morning, the hours of the Quarterly Examination being at that time from 8 to 12, A.M., and 2 to 4, P.M. Hutchinson was unquestionably very arbitrary and offensive in some of his regulations, but whether he was right or wrong he met the same cynical measure in "Pranceriana."[22]

---

[22] Other persons also were satirised occasionally in "Pranceriana," as, for instance, Philip Tisdall in the following description:—"He was a man formed by nature, and fashioned by long practice, for all manner of court intrigue. His stature was low, so as to excite neither envy nor observation; his countenance dismal, his public manners grave, and his address *humble*. But as in public he covered his prostitution by a solemnity of carriage, so in private he endeavoured to captivate by convivial humour, and to discountenance all public virtue by the exercise of a perpetual, and sometimes not unsuccessful, irony. To these qualifications he added an extraordinary magnificence of living.(1) His table was furnished with everything that splendour could suggest, or luxury could conceive, and his position and policy united to solicit a multitude of guests. To his house, then, resorted all those who wished through him to obtain, or learn from him to enjoy, without remorse, those public endowments which are the purchase of *public infidelity*." Tisdall was depicted in "Baratariana" also. In the pungent rhyme on "The rejection of the Altered Money Bill," in 1772, we have—

> "The next that stepped forward was innocent Phil,
> Who said 'that in things of the kind he'd no skill,
> But yet that he thought it a mighty good bill,'
> Which nobody can deny."

And again, in "A list of the Pack," we have—

> "Lo, Tisdall, whose looks would make honest men start,
> Who hangs out in his face the black sign of his heart;
> If you thought him no devil his aim he would miss,
> For he would, if he could, appear worse than he is.
> Then kick out these rascally knaves, boys;
> Freemen we will be to our graves, boys;
> Better be dead than be slaves, boys;
> A coffin or freedom for me."

Philip Tisdall enjoyed a long tenure of very distinguished success. He was educated at Sheridan's celebrated school in Capel-street, and thence entered Trinity College as a fellow-commoner in 1718. His Matriculation is:—"1718, Nov. 11th. Philip Tisdel. Soc. Com. Educatus Dub. Mag. Sheridan. (Tutor) Mr. Delany." He took his B.A. in the spring commencements of 1722, the shortened three-and-a-half years' academic course, as exemplified in the case of Grattan and Fitzgibbon [see note D], being a fellow-commoner's privilege. In 1739, Tisdall was elected simultaneously M.P. for Armagh and for the University. He chose the latter, and succeeded in a parliamentary petition against Alexander Macaulay. He afterwards contested the seat successfully in 1761 against Mr. French, Lord Clonmel's nominee; and in 1776 unsuccessfully against Provost Hutchinson's second son. In 1741, Tisdall was promoted Third-Serjeant, in 1751 he was Solicitor-General, and from 1761 till his death he was Attorney-General. In 1761 he was presented by the City of Cork with its freedom in a silver box. The Solicitor-General Gore was, in consequence of some of Tisdall's trimming, appointed over his head Chief Justice of the King's Bench, and soon after was created Lord Annaly. Tisdall was a very eminent lawyer, and although not at all an orator, he had great weight and influence in the House of Commons. He commenced political life as a patriot, and became the organ of the Junto. He was then, along with Pery and Hutchinson, bought

The "Lachrymæ," published in 1777, was the work of Dr. Duigenan alone (see note B), and in it he gives full fling to his hatred of the Provost. It is an able and envenomed indictment, and the author hits his victim with the utmost roughness. He accuses the Provost of violating every clause of the Provost's oath, and of being guilty of every possible abuse of his high office; he, moreover, defames Dr. Leland (see note C), and the other Fellows who were or became civil and courteous to the Provost. Duigenan acknowledges that he set himself to be insolent to the Provost; he tells what brave plans of defiance and revenge he formed, and how, after all, the Provost punished him and put him down.

The "Lachrymæ" records all this in piquant and entertaining fashion; and, besides being damaging to the Provost's character, it is interesting still as a sort of College Calendar of the period, giving antiquarian information of much value concerning the administration, economies, and discipline of the College a hundred years ago. It begins with reciting the naked and unprincipled manœuvre with Sir John Blacquiere, the Chief Secretary[23] to Lord Lieutenant Harcourt, by which Hutchinson, a layman, was appointed Provost, by virtue of the Crown's dispensing with the Statute which required the office to be filled by a Doctor or Bachelor in Divinity. Blacquiere's origin, Duigenan says, was like the source of the Nile, only to be guessed at, and Blacquiere himself was insolent, illiterate, and avaricious. On the death of Provost Andrews, in 1774, he recommended as his successor John Hely Hutchinson, who resigned in his patron's favour the office of Alnager, which Blacquiere ere long farmed out at £1,200 per annum.

by the corrupter, Lord Lieutenant Townshend. Tisdall's house was in Chancery-lane, and his country villa was in Stillorgan. He died in 1777. He was son of Richard Tisdall, Registrar in Chancery, and succeeded his father in the office, 1744. Philip's wife, Mary, had a pension of one hundred a year, and his brother Thomas was Registrar of the Court of Admiralty. In his will, made 1772, which is in the Public Record Office, he leaves a remembrance to his daughter, Elizabeth Morgan, "heretofore amply provided for." The whole of his real and personal estate he leaves to his wife Mary. His daughter Elizabeth, by his wife Mary (Singleton), niece and co-heiress of Lord Chief Justice Singleton, was baptised in St. Bride's Church. She was married to Colonel Morgan, of Cork Abbey, county Wicklow, and was grandmother to the late H. U. Tighe, Dean of Ardagh, and of the Chapel Royal, Dublin, and afterwards of Londonderry.—[Burke's Landed Gentry, Art., "Tighe of Mitchelstown;" Life of Charlemont. Life of Shelbourne, Record Office, and S. Bride's Register.]

(1) In the pre-Union times, when a home parliament secured the residence of our aristocracy and gentry, Dublin was famous for its fashion and hospitalities. Primate Stone maintained a lordly style at Leixlip Castle; while, as we read in "Mrs. Delany's Letters," Bishop Clayton at St. Woolstons, close by, and in St. Stephen's-green, kept up an equal grandeur. His house in the Green had a front like Devonshire House, and was *magnifique*. Mrs. Clayton's coach, with six flouncing Flanders mares, was not "out-looked by any equipage except the Duke of Dorset's, for she would not be outshone by her neighbours, a thing not easily done here." The Delanys entertained Viceroyalty at Delville, fed their own deer, and went about in a coach-and-six. Luke Gardiner's (Lord Mountjoy) house in the Phœnix Park was the head-quarters of fashionable life(a); and Hussey Burgh drove his coach-and-six, with outriders. The wealthy wool, linen, silk, &c., mercers, of Bride-street and Golden-lane, kept good style and equipages also, as appears by their wills in the Public Record Office.

(a) Gardiner was Master of the Revels, and Surveyor-General of Customs.
[23] See note E.

Duigenan says that whilst the bargain was in agitation Blacquiere represented the Provostship as much more valuable than it was. He adds that Hutchinson "complained loudly that he had been bitten," and that to make the best of a bad bargain he took in hands the College Estate.

Henry Flood was an eager candidate for the Provostship, and was put off with a vice-treasurership, and a salary of £3,500 a year. Blacquiere would have given him the Provostship if he could have paid a higher price than Hutchinson; and "he would have sold it to a chimney-sweeper if he had been the highest bidder." Duigenan says that all he knew of Flood was that he had been bought by Blacquiere, but he had no doubt that he would have made a better Provost than Hutchinson.[24] His disgust against Hutchinson is so intense that it overrides his sour nationality and his jealousy for the rights of the body to which he belonged; and he declares that he would have preferred the appointment of an Oxford or Cambridge clergyman.

In the *Gazette* announcement of Hutchinson's appointment his "LL.D." was puffed, but Duigenan strips the degree of all merit by explaining that it was only an "honorary" one—that it had no Academic significance—that every member of the Irish Parliament had a customary right to it—that it had just been conferred on an ignorant carpenter, one John Magill[25]—and that, as the climax of the prostitution, he himself, Duigenan, in his capacity of Regins Professor of Civil Law, had officially presented Blacquiere for the honour![26]

Non-fellow, unlearned, and layman as he was, Hutchinson got the Provostship, and he was not long in finding out that the constitution of the college afforded a sphere for energy which precisely suited him. By the "New Statutes," i.e., the Charter and Statutes drawn up by Archbishop Laud, the Provost possessed, or was supposed traditionally to possess,[27] almost absolutely, the management of the college estates, the disposal of its revenues, the nomination of fellows and scholars, and the power of rewarding and punishing fellows and scholars. The choice of parliamentary representatives for the University rested—not as since the Reform Act, with the registered Masters of Arts and Ex Scholars at large—with the corporate body of the fellows and scholars for the time being, all of whom were in a great degree subject to the statutable powers and underhand influence of the Provost. The body consisted of twenty-two fellows and seventy scholars. The Col-

---

[24] Flood, who did not get the provostship, bequeathed, by his will, in 1791, to the college, his estate in Kilkenny, worth £5,000 a year, to found and endow a professorship of the Erse or Irish language, and to establish a library of manuscripts and books in that language, and in the modern polished languages. Provost Hutchinson did not leave a shilling to the college. Flood's bequest fell through owing to his illegitimacy. He entered Trinity College as a fellow-commoner, completed his junior sophister terms, and then migrated *ad eundem* to Oxford.—[Flood's "Life of Flood," and Webb's "Com. Biog."]

[25] He was a Commissioner of Barracks; as was also Sir Herc. Langrishe. Langrishe was, besides, Commissioner of Revenue and Commissioner of Excise.

[26] There does not seem to have been any Mr. Barlow in these servile days to exercise the ancient tribunitial power of the Senior Master Non Regent—the power to veto, in the name of the community, dishonouring presentations to honorary degrees.

[27] See page xxxiii.

lege was the only asylum in the kingdom for friendless merit, and Duigenan knew five contemporary bishops who had been fellows.[28] All its usefulness and all its glories were swept away by the appointment of "Mr."—for he would not call him Dr.—Hutchinson.

Duigenan explains that it took five years' hard study to get a fellowship; that the juniors were subject to incessant toil and irksome bondage as tutors, and that their single compensating prospect was co-option. The income of the juniors was only £40 a year, but the seniors at that time handed over to them the pupils to help their scanty maintenances.[29] The "Natives' Places" were held by Scholars who were Irish born, and who succeeded to the Places by seniority and diligent attendance on college duties.

Sizarships were given by nomination, the Provost claiming eight nominations to one of each of the senior fellows, the previous system of election by examination having been superseded by Hutchinson. There was not one of these departments in which, according to Duigenan, Provost Hely Hutchinson did not traffic—and Duigenan's statements are borne out by the evidence before the parliamentary committee.[30] It was the same with "non-coing," i.e., allowing money in lieu of commons in the hall; the same in the matter of chambers, the same in regard of leaves of absence, the same in regard of fines, and the same in everything. In all these matters benefits were given to those who would vote for the Provost's sons, and rights were refused to those who would not so vote. The Fellows in those days used to have to purchase their rooms from the college—they could be compelled by the Provost to attend the lectures of the professors, and Duigenan says that the Provost once ordered him to leave the law courts to attend one of these lectures. Fellows had the right of visiting the students' rooms—they used to chum together—they used to be allowed to borrow money from the College, and under this arrangement Duigenan owed £300, while Leland and others owed more.

From the time of the "Glorious Revolution" none but Fellows had ever been

---

[28] In 1726, Primate Boulter wrote that unless a new Englishman was appointed to a then vacant bishopric there would be thirteen Irish bishops to nine English, to the Primate's great dismay. The Editor of "Boulter's Letters," in 1770, adds, in a note, that there was at one time in the Irish House of Lords a majority of native bishops, of whom five had been fellows of the University, viz., Drs. Howard, Synge, Clayton, Whitcombe (Archbishop of Cashel), and Berkeley. These are, probably, the five alluded to by Duigenan. In a pamphlet entitled "Thoughts on the Present State of the College of Dublin," published in 1782, the well-informed author says that in King William's reign, at or nearly at the same time, "the people saw ten prelates on the bench, who had been Fellows." The writer says that there was a great increase in the number of students—that the undergraduates were 565, the average of entrances 144 yearly, and the average of B.A. degrees, 78.—[*Halliday Collection.*]

We can ourselves remember, dating from the year 1830, eight bishops and one archbishop, all Ex-Fellows. Altogether "there have been seven archbishops and forty-two bishops of the Irish Church chosen from amongst the Fellows of Trinity College. Eight have become Members of Parliament, and six have been raised to the Judicial Bench."—[*Coll. Cal.*]

[29] This seems not to have been the case in Dr. Delany's time. See Primate Boulter's Letters, and Mrs. Delany's, and Swift's.

[30] See page xxviii, &c.

made Provosts, although during that period five Provosts had been appointed. Dr. Andrew's Fellowship was a sort of excuse for appointing him, although he was a layman; and Duigenan, in calculating the pecuniary losses which he sustained through Hutchinson, intimates that a similar dispensation might have been exercised towards himself if in due course he had succeeded to his Senior Fellowship. These losses he sets down at £3,000 actual, and £6,000 on the calculation of contingencies. The Provostship was worth £2,100 a year, besides a splendid residence. A Senior-Fellowship, we are told, was worth £700 a year; a Junior-Fellowship, including pupils, £200; Scholars had free commons, and there were thirty Native Places, with £20 a year each additional; the Beadle of the University had £20 a year; the Porters £5 a year, with clothes and food in the hall. On an average two Fellowships became vacant every three years. All these particulars Duigenan gives, and they all are made to serve as counts in his indictment of the Provost.

Hutchinson had the College estates surveyed, and Duigenan makes a grievous complaint of this proceeding. He says the survey cost the College two thousand pounds, and that it was an iniquitous device for raising the College rents upon improvements that had been effected by the tenants.[31] He declares that from the rent-raising there resulted beggary, discontent, and emigration. The renewal fines were divided into nine parts, of which two went to the Provost, and one to each of the seven seniors. In the year 1850, the fines were transferred to the College account, and the Senior Fellows were compensated out of the "Cista communis."[32]

The "LACHRYMÆ" tells how the Provost got the large old college plate melted down, and turned into a modern service, destroying the engraved coats-of-arms and names of the donors, at an expense to the college of £400.[33] He soon after had

----

[31] The rack-renting cannot have been very exorbitant, inasmuch as the average rent per acre now paid to the College by its perpetuity tenants is four shillings and twopence. The great bulk of the College property is situated in the counties of Armagh, Kerry, and Donegal. The following statement gives in round numbers the acreage and rental:—

	Acres.	Rent.	Rent per acre.	
Armagh,	23,000	£9,600	8s.	4d.
Kerry,	60,000	11,500	3s.	10d.
Donegal,	62,700	9,000	2s.	10d.
Total,	145,700	£30,100	4s.	2d.

The number of perpetuity holdings let by the College are in all fifty-four; four only are let to persons of the class of tenant-farmers; of the remaining fifty, sixteen, containing over 60,000 acres, are enjoyed by three lessees, who pay the College an average rent of 3s. 5d. per acre.—[See Letter by Rev. J. A. Galbraith, S.F.T.C.D., Bursar, *Freeman's Journal*, March 6, 1882, and also "Statement to the Chief Secretary."—*Freeman*, March, 15, 1882.]

[32] The renewal fines in 1850 averaged £6,700 a year. The arbitration at that time between the College and the tenants cost the College £3,000.—[See Letter by Rev. T. Stack, S.F.T.C.D., Registrar, printed in the Report of the Bessborough Commission, and also "Statement" as above.]

[33] This charge, as it stands, rests on a slender foundation, and is very misleading. The catalogue of the College plate, which, to guard against such imputations in future, Mr.

it moved out to Palmerston House, and Duigenan does not seem to feel at all sure about its honest return. Most of the Fellows were in the Provost's power by being married, and Duigenan says that he used the power tyrannically.[34] A Fellow going out on a living was allowed only five months' benefit of salary.[35]

Duigenan seems to hold the Provost responsible for the "mean and decayed" condition of the chapel, and he more than once rails at him for being of mean parentage.[36] He finds that since the time of Charles I. no Provost, except Hutchin-

Hingston, the Chief Steward, has drawn up with so much care and skill, shows that the old inscribed plate is still in use; and it enumerates pieces dated as early as 1632 and 1638. A selection of the service was sent over, in Mr. Hingston's charge, to the late South Kensington Exhibition, and was greatly admired by all who were conversant with antique silver art—some of the choicest pieces being facsimiled for the London Institution. The collection of plate is abundant, and the store was accumulated in this way. It used to be the custom that all students at entrance should deposit "caution money," which was returned to them on graduation. The rich men and Fellow Commoners, instead of taking back the money, used to present it to the College in the form of inscribed goblets or tankards, and in the course of years there was a large assortment of these offerings. Provost Hutchinson had a number of these tankards melted down and refashioned into the present silver plates, and this he did with the consent of the Board. Before Hutchinson's time a large quantity of the plate was sold by the Board, and the produce was invested in the purchase of land. In 1689, when James II. seized on the College, the Vice-Provost and Fellows sold £30 worth of the plate for subsistence of themselves and the Scholars. At the same time all the rest of the plate was seized on and taken away to the Custom House by Col. Luttrel, King James's Governor of the city, but it was preserved and afterwards restored to the College.—[See Mr. Hingston's Catalogue and *Coll. Cal.* List of Fellows, 1689.]

[34] In 1775, seven marriage dispensations by King's Letters were obtained.—[Lib. Mun.]

[35] In 1796, the term of grace was extended to a twelvemonth by a King's Letter.—[Lib. Mun.]

[36] The following—the 5th verse in Milliken's ever popular song, "The Groves of Blarney"—was an *impromptu* addition at an electioneering dinner in the south of Ireland in 1798. It is said to have been intended as an insult to Lord Donoughmore, who was present, but his Lordship's readiness completely turned the tables. He applauded the verse, and in a humorous speech acknowledged the relationship, thanked the author, and toasted the Murphy's, Clearys, Helys, and others who in the recent political contest had ventured life and limb in support of the Hutchinson cause, and had thus made their blood-relationship with him unquestionable.

> "'Tis there's the kitchen hangs many a flitch in,
> With the maids a stitching upon the stair;
> The bread and biske', the beer and whiskey,
> Would make you frisky if you were there.
> 'Tis there you'd see Peg Murphy's daughter
> A washing *praties* forenint the door,
> With Roger Cleary, and Father Healy,
> All blood relations to my Lord Donoughmore.
> Oh, Ullagoane."

Lord Hutchinson always heartily enjoyed this verse, which has become completely identified with Milliken's song.—(See Crofton Croker's "Popular Songs of Ireland," pp. 144-8.)

son and his predecessor, had ever sat in the House of Commons. He is obliged to admit that Dr. Andrews' conduct in private life was somewhat too loose and unguarded for a Provost; but still he was better than Hutchinson, though he was told that the latter was a good husband and father. Mr. Hutchinson might be a good husband and father, "but no one would think the better of a wolf because the beast was kind to its mate and cubs." Hutchinson had destroyed the seclusion and retirement of the college by infesting its walks and gardens with his wife, adult daughters, infant children with nurses and go-carts, and military officers on prancing horses. He had endeavoured to institute a riding-school and a professorship of horsemanship after the example of Oxford, and he had desecrated the Convocation or Senate Hall by making it a fencing-school. Duelling had become the fashion among the students under the influence of the Provost's evil example, and the college park was made the ground for pistol practice.[37]

We are told further by Duigenan that the number of students then on the college books was 598, of whom 228 were intern.[38] We see by the *Liber Munerum Hiberniæ* that by 1792 the number of students had so much increased, consequently on the liberal education spirit of Grattan's parliament, that a King's Letter was obtained raising the quarterly examination days from two to four. In the following year was the King's Letter directing the admission of Catholics to degrees on taking the oath of Abjuration and Allegiance, in accordance with the Act of the Irish Parliament, and in 1794 appears the first "R. C." entry (Thomas Fitzgerald, of Limerick) on the College Matriculation Books. From that date onward the religious denomination of pupils has always been recorded.

"Pranceriana," i.e., probably Duigenan, asserts that the Provost, on the eve of the second election in which his son was returned, offered to supply to a voter amongst the candidates for Fellowship a copy of the questions which he was to give in Moral Science for the ensuing examinations;[39] and Duigenan openly says that the Provost was determined that no one should be elected a Scholar who would not previously promise to vote as he should direct him.

He kept an electioneering agent inside the walls, a spy and a corrupter, — "in short, the Blacquiere of Mr. Hutchison." Duigenan gives a long list of the Provost's insolences to himself and to other members of the body. He resisted marriage dispensations to the Fellows who were his opponents, while he procured them for his creatures — Leland and Dabzac.

Father Prout has not translated this verse. Why does not Professor Tyrrell render it, *Græce et Latine?*

[37] He challenged Mr. Doyle to single combat for daring to issue an address to the University constituency against his (the Provost's) son's candidature. Mr. Doyle was a helpless invalid at the time, and had to stand on a spread-out coat, for fear of cold; the combatants met on Summer-hill, "fired a pistol each, and made up the matter without blood." Hutchinson had previously challenged Dr. Lucas, the patriot, who was crippled with rheumatism.

[38] The number now is 1,338, of whom 789 are "Residents" —*i.e.,* living within reach of College opportunities. [See Dr. Haughton's return analysis, quoted in the *Freeman's Journal* of January 7, 1882.] The number of students on the books under the degree of M.A. is 1,253 [see *College Calendar* for 1882, page 434]. The number of interns now is 250.

[39] See page xxviii.

On the death of Shewbridge the Fellow, which was attributed to Hutchison's refusing him leave to go to the country for change of air, the students defied the Provost's order for a private interment at 6 o'clock in the morning. They had the bell rung, had a night burial and a torchlight procession, attended the funeral in mourning, and afterwards broke into the Provost's house.

In the first year of his office the Provost dispersed a meeting of the Scholars and some of the Fellows that was held by advertisement at Ryan's in Fownes-street, "the principal tavern in the city," for the purpose of nominating candidates for the representation of the University against the Provost's nominees.

Duigenan goes on to relate how Hutchinson discharged the various duties of the high office which he had acquired by the traffic above stated. He made an exhibition of his ignorance at a Fellowship Examination by suggesting that Alexander the Great died in the time of the Peloponessian War; but ridiculous a figure as he made in the Scholarship and Fellowship Examinations, he would not withdraw from them, because unless he examined he could not vote or nominate at the election of the Scholars and Fellows. This nomination power was with him a darling object in the execution of his electioneering projects of making the College a family borough, and he abstained from no methods to effectuate his scheme.

We are told at length how the Provost, with the consent of a majority of the Board, deprived Berwick of his Scholarship for absence, because Berwick would not vote for his son, and how the Visitors, on appeal, restored him.[40] How he deprived Mr. Gamble of the buttery clerkship, and replaced him, on the threat of an appeal, suggested and drawn up by Duigenan. How the Provost refused Mr. FitzGerald, a Fellow, leave to accompany his sick wife to the country, and tried to provoke FitzGerald's hot temper. The Provost's cruelties and injuries to Duigenan himself knew no limits. He says, that for the purpose of keeping him from being co-opted, the Provost had the Board Registry falsified, that he set the porters to watch him, that he persecuted him, and mulcted him in the buttery books, for sleeping out of college without leave. He relates that he was attacked by the Provost's gang, and was obliged in consequence to wear arms; and that, finally, Hutchinson compelled him to go out on the Laws' Professorship on a salary which was raised to £460 a year.[41]

The "Lachrymæ Academicæ" shows how Duigenan spent the leisure hours of his enforced retirement.

It was dedicated to King George III. Duigenan had "dragged this Cacus (the

[40] On this Visitation "Pranc. Poet." has—

> "Disgrac'd by libels, worried by his foes
> Poor Prancer labours under endless woes;
> He therefore only supplicates your Grace
> That right or wrong you'll keep him in his place."

The Visitation lasted five days, and was held before Primate Robinson as Vice-Chancellor for the Duke of Gloucester, and Archbishop Cradock of Dublin. Hutchinson published a pamphlet reviling the Visitors, and pronouncing their decision invalid.

[41] A King's Letter was obtained for raising the salary for this special occasion.—*Lib. Mun.*

Provost) from his den," and he appealed to the Duke of Gloucester as Chancellor, and to the archbishops of Armagh and Dublin as Visitors, to rescue the college out of the hands of this worse than Vandalic destroyer, this molten calf, and paste-board Goliath. As this remedy might fail, from the uncertainty of all events in this world, Duigenan pointed out two other remedies, the application of which lay with the King. One was to have the Provost's patent voided by a *scire facias*, and the other was to deprive him of all power, authority, or revenue in the college, during his life. His authority was to be transferred to the Board, and his revenue to be appropriated to pay for the new building. These suggestions were not adopted, but the *Lachrymæ* did not by any means fall still-born from the press. It produced a powerful sensation within the walls and in outer circles.

On the 19th of July it was censured by the Board in the following resolution:—

"Whereas, a pamphlet hath lately been published in the city of Dublin, with the title of "Lachrymæ Academicæ," to which the name of Patrick Duigenan, LL.D., is prefixed as author, traducing the character of the Right Honourable the Provost and some respectable Fellows of this society, and misrepresenting and vilifying the conduct of the said Provost and Fellows, and the government of the said college, without regard to truth or decency.

"Resolved by the Provost and Senior Fellows that the author and publishers of the said pamphlet shall be prosecuted in the course of law, and that orders to that purpose be given to the law agent of the college.

"Ordered that the said resolution be published in the English and Irish newspapers."—[*Extract from College Register, July 19, 1777.*]

The censure was officially published in the *Dublin Journal*, and in *Saunders' News Letter*; whereupon Duigenan inserted in the *Freeman* the following advertisement:—

"Whereas, a false and malicious advertisement has been inserted in the *Dublin Journal*, and in *Saunders' News Letter*, containing a resolution of the Board of Trinity College, Dublin, relative to a book written and published by me, entitled, 'Lachrymæ Academicæ; or, the present deplorable state of the College of the Holy and undivided Trinity, of Queen Elizabeth, near Dublin.' It is necessary to inform the public that the said resolution was carried at the Board by the votes of Drs. Leland, Dabzac, Wilson, and Forsayeth (the very same persons who voted for the unstatutable deprivation of Mr. Berwick), against the opinions of Mr. Clement, the Vice-Provost, of Dr. Murray, and Dr. Kearney. It is also necessary to observe that three of these gentlemen who voted for the above resolution are persons whom I have declared my intention, in my book, of accusing, before the Visitors, of having committed unstatutable crimes; which intention I shall most certainly execute.[42] And I do hereby pledge myself to the public that I will effectually prosecute at law

[42] Duigenan did not execute this intention, as appears by the following record, kindly supplied by Dr. Carson, S.F.T.C.D.:—"I have to inform you that I have gone carefully through the College Register for the years 1777 and 1778, and I cannot find therein the least trace of any Visitation having been held in either of these years. The censure on Dr. Duigenan is duly recorded under its proper date, in the year 1777; but no further Collegiate notice appears to have been taken of it."

every one of the junto for the said scurrilous advertisement, and the resolution therein contained.

"PAT. DUIGENAN,

"Chancery Lane, July 21st, 1777."

"N.B.—Dr. Murray signed the said advertisement officially as Registrar of the College, who is obliged to sign resolutions of the majority of the Board. He strenuously opposed the resolution therein contained, and the insertion of it in the Public Prints."

Besides these Board proceedings, the "Lachrymæ" led to a plentiful crop of litigation in the Courts. In Michaelmas Term, 1777, in the King's Bench, Serjeant Wood moved for an information against Duigenan at the suit of the Provost on account of the defamation in the "Lachrymæ," and the application was granted. The same time Barry Yelverton, on the part of Dr. Arthur Browne, Fellow, and Member for the University, moved for an information against the *Hibernian Journal*, and Fitzgibbon moved for informations against two persons for challenging Duigenan. Applications granted.

In 1778 Counsellors Smith, Burgh, &c., showed cause on behalf of Dr. Duigenan against making absolute the Rule for information against the "Lachrymæ," when Judge Robinson dismissed the case, saying that it had already taken up fifteen days of the public time, and that he "left the School to its own correctors."[43]

In 1776, Duigenan insulted the Provost in the Four Courts, and the Provost, disdaining Duigenan, called upon Tisdall to make him responsible for his follower's conduct. He told Tisdall to consider that he had insulted him with a view to provoke a challenge. This was the occasion on which Duigenan threatened to bulge the Provost's eye. Tisdall at once applied for an information against him in the King's Bench. Seventeen counsel were engaged in the cause.

Hutchinson argued his own case before the Court with consummate ability. He delivered a most masterly speech, and offered an apology for calling Tisdall an old scoundrel and an old rascal. He did not recollect having used these expressions, but if he did use them, it was out of Court. He referred pathetically to all the annoyance and ridicule that he was undergoing by pamphlets and in the public press; and he excused his appearing in his own defence by the circumstance that his lawyers were harassed in attendance on the six different suits promoted against him on very unaccountable motives.

The Court of King's Bench made the rule against him absolute, but the proceedings collapsed in consequence of Tisdall's death.[44]

Duigenan says that Hutchinson was once publicly chastised by a gentleman whom he had affronted, but we have no other account of the circumstance. Duigenan makes out that he was a coward as well as a tyrant and impostor, and he compares him to "Cacofogo," the usurer in Beaumont and Fletcher's play.

In 1789, the Provost supported Grattan in the Regency Bill, and in the motions

[43] Walker's Hiber. Mag. 177-8.
[44] Grattan's Life, and *Hib. Mag.*

connected with it. For this he was liable to be dismissed from the lucrative offices which he held under the Crown, and to save himself from this penalty he signed the "Round Robin" of the twenty peers and thirty-seven commoners who were in a similar predicament. This famous instrument which was drawn up in the Provost's house, pledged the co-signers to stand or fall together, and bound them as a body "to make Government impossible" if the Viceroy, Lord Buckingham, were to venture to punish any of them. Fitzgibbon, then Attorney-General, mercilessly crushed and humbled the "Parliamentary Whiteboys;" he made the synagogue of Satan come and worship before his feet,[45] and the most abject of the recreants was the Provost.[46]

To secure the control of the parliamentary representation of the University was, as has been said, one of Hutchinson's dearest plans. The pursuit of it led him, according to all accounts, into some of his most dishonourable and vindictive actions, and after all he won but temporary and chequered success in the ambitious experiment. In the prosecution of these election aims, the Provost stuck at nothing. He had agents and emissaries everywhere; and through them as well as by his own direct efforts he instituted an all-pervading system of corruption. He knew how to make subtle but palpable advances to the voters that were under his eye, and to tamper at the same time with their friends and parents at a distance. He ransacked every department of Academic life so as to be expert at turning the whole system of collegiate rewards and punishments into an organised instrumentality for bribery. All the emoluments, rewards, and conveniences of the college were reserved for those who promised their vote to the Provost, and all the obsolete and vexatious disciplines were enforced against those who were disposed to assert their independence in exercising the franchise. By an unscrupulous use of both his patronage, and his powers as Returning Officer, he was enabled to get two of his sons returned for the University, but he saw powerful and damaging petitions against both of them. In 1776, he returned his eldest son Richard against Tisdall, the Attorney-General. Tisdall lodged a petition in June, which the House ordered to be considered in July, but before that day the Parliament was prorogued, and did not meet again till October in the following year. Meanwhile, Tisdall died; the petition was moved by Madden and King, and ultimately, in March, 1778, the Select Committee unseated Hutchinson. John Fitzgibbon conducted the petition, and thereby established his position as a lawyer. He was elected for the University in Hutchinson's room, and the foundation of his coming greatness was laid.[47]

[45] The Round Robiners probably bethought of the case of 1753 when the patriots who resisted the Court in the matter of the disposal of surplus revenue were dismissed from office by Primate Stone. They, no doubt, were afterwards reinstated with honour, but the conspirators of 1789 had to deal with John Fitzgibbon. — [See "Plowden," p. 311, &c.]

[46] Froude, vol. ii., p. 509.

[47] Barry Yelverton was an unsuccessful candidate in this College Election of 1776. In the next year he was elected for Donegal, Belfast, and Carrickfergus, and chose the last. — [*Ho. Co. Jour.*]

It was as Recorder of Carrickfergus that Barry Yelverton presented Hussey Burgh with an address and the freedom of that Corporation in a gold box for resisting the Government on the question of Supplies while Prime Serjeant, and losing his place thereby. [*Freeman's Journal*, Jan. 4, 1780.]

Richard Hutchinson, it maybe observed, fell back on Sligo, to which he had been elected at the same time that he was elected for the University, and where he seems to have escaped another petition by choosing the University constituency. In the debate as to whether a new writ should be issued for Sligo, in 1778, the Provost took a forward part, and bewailed that he "was forced to go there out of his sick bed to defend his son." The Gravamina of the College petition of 1778 were almost identical with those of the petition of 1790, and while Parliament was unseating the Provost's son, the Court of Common Pleas was dealing with the Provost himself. The Rev. Edward Berwick, whose case is related in the "Lachrymæ," took an action against the Returning Officer for refusing his vote. The Court, overruling the Provost's objection, made an order that the Plaintiff should have liberty to inspect all the College books that could be of use to him in his suit. The verdict was against the defendant, without costs.[48]

After the disastrous parliamentary petition of 1778, the Provost took no family part in the College elections until the year 1790, when his second son Francis was returned. His return led to a parliamentary inquiry; and the case, which is fully reported, is a very interesting passage in the history of the College and of Hutchinson.[49]

The committee, consisting of fourteen members, besides the chairman, W. Burston, Esq., was chosen on the 14th day of Feb., 1791, and on it sat, amongst the others, the Hon. Arthur Wesley (Duke of Wellington), Right Hon. Lord Edward Fitzgerald, and Right Hon. Denis Daly.

There were two petitions, one by Laurence Parsons, Esq., the defeated candidate, and the other by some scholars and other electors of the borough. The sitting member was the Hon. Francis Hely Hutchinson, and the returning officer was his father the Provost. There was a powerful bar. Beresford Burston, Michael Smith (afterwards Master of the Rolls), Peter Burrowes, and William Conyngham Plunket, were for the petitioners; Tankerville Chamberlain (afterwards Judge of the Queen's Bench), and Luke Fox (afterwards judge), were for the sitting member; and Robert Boyd (afterwards Judge of King's Bench), and Denis George, Recorder of Dublin (and afterwards Baron of the Exchequer), were for the Provost. The total constituency was 92, and out of these "84 and no more" tendered their votes. Arthur Browne was returned at the head of the poll by 62 votes, Parsons had 43, and Hutchinson 39. The Provost, on the scrutiny, reduced Browne's votes to 51, Parsons' to 34, and his son's to 36, thus returning his son by a majority of two over Parsons. Against this return the petitioners set forth that the Provost received for his son the votes of several persons who had no right to vote; that he refused for Parsons the votes of several who were legally entitled to vote; that on the scrutiny, he received illegal evidence; that he acted as agent for his son, and by undue means procured votes for him; that he exerted his prerogative antecedently to the election for the purpose of illegally influencing the electors; and that by illegal and partial scrutiny he reduced the number of the votes for Parsons below the number

---

[48] *Walker's Hibernian Magazine, Freeman's Journal,* and *Exshaw's Magazine.*

[49] "The case of the Borough of Trinity College, near Dublin, as heard before a Select Committee of the House of Commons, A.D. 1791."

of the votes for his son. Burston stated the case, and referred to the election of 1776, when the Provost's eldest son was unseated for undue influence. He gave numerous instances of the Provost's abuse of his powers in the matters of "non-coing" and leaves of absence. He complained of his rejecting votes on the ground of minority on the evidence chiefly of the Matriculation-book. Amongst the witnesses examined were the Very Rev. Wensley Bond, Sch., 1761, Dean of Ross; G. Miller, Fellow (and afterwards Master of Armagh Royal School); William Magee, Fellow and Junior Dean (and afterwards Archbishop of Dublin); Toomy, a scholar (and afterwards Professor of Medicine); Dr. Marsh, Fellow, and Registrar of the college; Whitly Stokes, Fellow (and afterwards Professor of Physic), &c. &c.

The examination of the witnesses brought out a great many curious and interesting facts relative to college men and college administration a hundred years ago. For instance, Mr. Fox, in arguing against the right of Scholars, being minors, to vote, referred to the election of 1739, when Alexander MacAulay, Dean Swift's nominee,[50] was elected against Philip Tisdall; and when the election was set aside by the House of Commons on account of the vote of Mr. Sullivan[51] (afterwards Professor of Laws), who, being elected a Fellow at nineteen years of age in 1738, was a minor when he voted.

Plunket and Smith argued on the other side that Scholars, being minors, were entitled to their votes, and that these votes were allowed in the contested election of 1761, when Lord Clonmel ran French against the Attorney General, Tisdall, on account of the latter's hesitancy about the Octennial Bill. It was argued further that the Matriculation-book was not legal evidence as to age, inasmuch as "boys without any sanction gave in their ages older than they really were, from a desire to be thought men." Finally, the committee resolved unanimously that Fellows and Scholars, though minors, have a right to vote for members to represent the University.

Mr. Miller[52] deposed that he was applied to by the Provost for his vote, and that he was offered a copy of the Provost's fellowship examination questions in Morality,[53] "an advantage," said Burrowes, "which would have made a docile

[50] Swift made an eager canvass for MacAulay, and wrote to Pope, asking him to write to Lord George (then Mr.) Lyttleton, who was private secretary to Frederick, Prince of Wales, the Chancellor of the University. The prince complied with the request, and Tisdall's supporters sent over a remonstrance. — ["Swift's Letters."]

[51] This Francis Stoughton Sullivan got Scholarship, in 1744, at fifteen, and was probably one of the youngest Scholars and the youngest Fellow in the college records.

[52] He published, through the University Press, in 1797, a scholarly Edition of "Longinus," and was the author of several other works. (See an interesting sketch of his life prefixed to Bohn's edition of his "Philosophy of History.")

[53] "About a month ago considerable sensation was created in Oxford by the rumour that one of the University examiners, who is also a "coach," had prepared his private pupils in the precise questions set for examination. This, we may observe, was one of the heavy charges brought against Provost Hely Hutchinson, of Trinity College, about a century ago, the Provost having had recourse to the unprincipled manœuvre as an electioneering dodge. The ever-memorable Counsellor Peter Burrowes, when arraigning the Provost before a committee of the Irish House of Commons, said that his trick "would have made a docile parrot appear superior to Sir Isaac Newton;" but the committee condoned the Provost,

parrot appear superior to Sir Isaac Newton." Three of the senior fellows voted for Hutchinson at the election. Toomey, a Scholar, was a Catholic, and refused to vote because the Junior Fellows could prove that he was a Catholic, and would take his pupils from him. He would not conform, although the Provost's eldest son pressed him, and told him that his own ancestors were Catholics and had conformed, and that he himself would be a Catholic if he lived in a Catholic country. Toomey knew that Casey, a Scholar, was a Catholic, and that he was chapel roll-keeper, attended college chapel twenty times a week, and partook of the Sacrament. Toomey "did not vote at the election because his vote would be of no use as he was a Roman Catholic."[54] James Hely, a Scholar, was a Catholic in Limerick, and had conformed in St. Werburgh's Church, in Dublin, to the Rev. Mr. L'Estrange, curate. The petitioners strove to disqualify Hely "for Popery," but his conformity was admitted by the committee.

Mr. Graves, Fellow (afterwards Professor of Divinity and Dean of Ardagh), had voted for Hutchinson, and he believed that the Provost did declare to the Senior Fellows that he would nominate him to the Fellowship even against the majority of the Board. Dr. Hales' pupils were worth £500 or £600 a year to him;[55] and on his resignation the Provost claimed the power of distributing his pupils amongst the other Fellows. Hales had sixty or seventy pupils. Fellow-commoners against the judgment and votes of Arthur Wesley (Duke of Wellington) and Lord Edward Fitzgerald. The Oxford authorities seem not to be disposed to view so leniently the action of Mr. Philip Aldred, D.C.L. When the matter was reported to the Vice-Chancellor a substitute for the transgressing examiner was at once appointed. We believe that a University committee has been appointed to consider the expediency of taking away Mr. Aldred's degrees—as was done in the Tractarian controversy days with Mr. Ward, the author of the "Ideal;" and, meanwhile, Mr. Aldred is now about to bring his case before the public, with the protest that he has been condemned unheard, after challenging investigation, and that he is able and willing to meet every charge brought against him."—[*Freeman's Journal*, Jan. 13th, 1882.]

[54] He was prevented from voting, not by any University or College statute, but by the Penal Law of 1727, which took away the franchise from Catholics. All the long past exclusiveness of the college, detrimental as it was to the college and to the country, was enjoined by the foreign power which cared little for the advancement of either. Down to this period the English legislature did not recognise at all the existence of Catholics in the college, believing them to be effectually excluded by the statute enforcing attendance at Anglican worship and Sacrament, and by the Supremacy and anti-Transubstantiation Declarations for Degrees, which were swept away by the Act of 1792.

[55] In 1725, Primate Boulter estimated that Dr. Delany, a Senior Fellow, and "the greatest pupil-monger," had from Fellowship and pupils six or seven hundred pounds per annum.—[*Letters*.]

Swift, in 1730, computed that Delany, "by the benefit of the pupils, and his Senior Fellowship, with all its perquisites, received every year between nine hundred and a thousand pounds."—[*Works*, vol. xiii., p. 82.]

Duigenan, in 1777, reckoned Dr. Leland's Senior Fellowship at "£800, one year with another."—[*Lachrymæ*.]

In 1777, it was considered surprising that Dr. Leland refused the living of Benburb, worth £1,000 a year, while his college income fell short of £700 a year.—[*Exshaw's Magazine*, 1777.]

paid £12, pensioners £6, per annum. It was deposed by another witness that the Provost nominated Mr. Ussher to a Fellowship in 1790—and it is so stated in the Calendar—although he had but two votes amongst the Senior Fellows, and those two were Drs. Kearney and Barrett.

Mr. Magee, Junior Dean, stated, that after his election to Fellowship he was desirous to go to the bar, and that the dispensation was prevented by the Provost. Shortly before the election, however, the Provost offered to obtain the dispensation for him, with commons money and the usual allowance, if he would either vote for Hutchinson or go out of the way. Magee declined both proposals, and lost the dispensation; but probably he got on as well in the Church as he would have succeeded at the Bar. In the course of Mr. Magee's examination the following passage occurred: "Counsel—Is not Dr. Fitzgerald a warm man? Magee—There are other warm men in college besides Dr. Fitzgerald. Counsel—I perceive there are." Mr. Toomy, a Scholar of the house, acknowledged that he was a Catholic. He told about "Regulators' Places" for Sizars, worth about £16 a year, and about "Natives' Places" for Scholars worth the same, and the electioneering use which the Provost made of these appointments. Mr. Stordy, the college clerk, told a great deal about the system of "non-coing." A Scholar's non-co was worth £16 a year, and a Fellow's was worth, for one half year, 7s. 7d. a week, and for the other half, 8s. 6d. a week, or about £21 a year. Dr. Marsh, Senior Fellow, was twice refused leave of absence by the Provost. The Provost gave the Vice-Chancellor's rooms to his own supporters. A Scholar could have leave for thirty-two days, and a fellow for sixty-three.[56] By Yelverton's Act, Trinity College students could be called to the bar three years before non-graduates.

Mr. Whitley Stokes, Fellow, gave instances of the Provost's partiality at the election.

Mr. Fox opened the case for the sitting Member, and maintained that there was no instance of undue influence, and he was followed by Mr. Boyd on the part of the Provost. Then Mr. Plunkett spoke to evidence, against the Provost and the sitting Member. The Recorder replied for the Provost in very eulogistic terms, mentioning his seven Under-Graduate premiums, his college reforms, improvements, &c. He disparaged the made-up arithmetical evidence of Miller and Magee, and was followed by Mr. Chamberlaine for the sitting Member. Mr. Burrowes closed the argument in a very eloquent speech, which was as severe on the Provost

---

[56] In 1713, Swift wrote to Stella:—"I have been employed in endeavouring to save one of your Junior Fellows (Mr. Charles Grattan) who came over here for a dispensation from taking orders, and in soliciting it has run out his time, and now his Fellowship is void if the College pleases, unless the queen suspends the execution and gives him time to take Orders. I spoke to all the ministers about it yesterday; but they say, 'the queen is angry and thought it but a trick to deceive her;' and she is positive, and so the man must be ruined, for I cannot help him. I never saw him in my life, but the case was so hard, I could not forbear interposing. Your Government recommended him to the Duke of Ormond, and he thought they would grant it; and by the time it was refused, the Fellowship by rigour is forfeited." The College Calendar has, "Charles Grattan, Fellow, 1710—removed for not taking Holy Orders, May 25th, 1713—Master of Enniskillen School, 1714."—[*Journal*, Letter lxii., March 29th.]

as the "Lachrymæ" or "Pranceriana" was. It is noticeable, by the way, that Duigenan took no part in the petitions, and that he was neither employed in the case
nor even named in the examination. Burrowes said that Miller's rejection of the
Provost's offer of his questions was "a moral miracle." It was Miller's third attempt
for fellowship.

Burrowes "lamented the necessity of the odious investigation which exposed
to public view the disgraceful and disastrous state of the University—condon-
ing the undue influence would make the college as corrupt as any pot-walloping
borough—the University would be shortly depopulated, and its only remaining
trace would be the octennial convention of an unresisted Provost, and unresisting
electors, to return suitable representatives to Parliament, and celebrate the festival
of banished literature and vanquished public spirit. The decay of the University in
such an event, would be desirable; its honours ought to be a brand of disgrace in
society, and the contaminated Scholar ought to become a despised and abandoned
citizen." Burrowes was full of pride and loyalty for the old place. He was himself
an Ex-Scholar,[57] as were also amongst the lawyers in the case Beresford Burston,
Plunket, Smith, Fox, and Boyd; and he was jealous for the honour of the Academic
prize. "Some of the most important officers in the state," he exclaimed, "are filled
by men who were Scholars of the University; in the learned professions the most
eminent men have in their youth been Scholars. The most respectable divines, the
most eminent lawyers, a considerable number of the Judges of the land, have been
Scholars. Every individual of the eight lawyers[58] who appeared before this Committee have been Scholars of the University."[59] Burrowes closed his speech:—"I
sit down assured you cannot pronounce the Honourable Francis Hely Hutchison
to have been duly elected." Forty-one witnesses were produced by the petitioners,
of whom ten were Fellows and thirteen Scholars. The Hutchisons produced six
witnesses—no Fellow, one Scholar, and a lady.

The Committee sat from the 14th February to the 24th March, when, by a
majority of one, including the double vote of the chairman, it resolved (Wellington and Lord E. Fitzgerald voting in the minority) "That the Hon. Francis Hely
Hutchinson had made use of no undue influence; that he was duly elected a bur-
gess to represent the University in the present Parliament; and that the Provost,
as Returning Officer of the University, acted legally and impartially at and before
the election."

Perhaps the most significant fact evolved by the investigation was that some

---

[57] He got Scholarship along with his brother Robert, in 1775. The brothers Roberts,
the present Senior Fellows, did the same in 1836.

[58] Denis George's name does not appear in the list of scholars. He took his B.A. in
1773. Neither does Tankerville Chamberlain's. He graduated in 1774.

[59] From the ranks of the Scholars have proceeded 13 Provosts, 199 Fellows; 1 Archbishop; 16 Bishops, of whom two held English sees; 4 Lord Chancellors; 2 Lords Justices; 29
Judges; 27 M.P.'s; 4 Vice-Chancellors; 18 Deans; 14 Governors, &c., of British dependencies;
renowned Professors in all the Faculties, and nearly all the distinguished schoolmasters of
the country; 1 Poet Laureate, and several celebrated authors and editors, besides numerous
eminent clergymen and lawyers. This is exclusive of the enumeration [page xviii] of the
dignities obtained by Scholar-Fellows.

of the Scholars were Catholics, the Statutes and the Anglican Sacrament notwithstanding. There was no reserve in the statement, and no remark on it was made by any member of Committee.[60] The point was not brought forward in the petition, nor pressed by any of the Council, except in the case of one Scholar, whose conformity was accepted by the Committee. In fact the "Popery" seems to have been taken quite as an understood thing,[61] and this coincides entirely with the famous declaration of Fitzgibbon. In 1782, speaking on Gardiner's Bill, in the Irish House of Commons, as Member for the University, he asserted that "the University of Dublin was already open, by connivance, and that no religious conformity was required." It is not easy to reconcile this with the then existing regulations for students as well as for Scholars, and in that debate the Provost did not speak exactly in this strain. On the contrary, he lamented that the religious disabilities did exist, and he was urgent for a King's Letter to give the Catholics equality in the University, under a Theological Professor of their own.[62]

That debate, it may be noticed, is memorable for the cordial and consenting speeches of the Provost and of the two Members for the University, Hussey Burgh and Fitzgibbon. They all were in favour of Catholic relief, especially in the matter of education, and they all would have opened the College freely and liberally to Catholics. It was in this debate that Hussey Burgh protested against the Irish Bishops' practice of ordaining men on Scotch degrees. The Provost warmly thanked Burgh for sustaining the right and the dignity of the University. He said that the number of yearly degrees had risen from 95 to 109, and that Trinity College Graduates could be supplied for as many curacies as had the legal allowance of £50 a year.[63]

Plunket was very indignant at the miserable bribery and corruption that were administered by the Provost, but he had not a word to say against the deeper and wider corruption that was ingrained in the sectarian exclusiveness of the constitution of the place. How could he say anything, being himself in the same condemnation? He was the son of a Unitarian minister;[64] and is said to have lived and died an Unitarian, and still he was a Scholar of the House.

In 1790, a very able pamphlet, suggested by Provost Hutchison's despotic *regime, was published* anonymously, entitled: "An Inquiry how far the Provost of

[60] It is even more remarkable that this matter was not mentioned by Duigenan.

[61] In the petition of 1778 one of the points set forth was that Scholars and Fellows should be legal Protestants to entitle them to vote, whereas the Provost had received for his son and Yelverton the votes of some who were not Protestants at the time of their election.

[62] Catholics and Nonconformists were not excluded from Scholarship by the statutes or by any oath. They were, however, designedly, and in the main effectually, excluded by the statute that all scholars, students, and sizars should attend chapel and partake of Holy Communion as often as it was administered (see "History of University," *Coll. Cal.*, 1876, vol. ii. p. 9), and the "Heron Visitation" (Chartæ and Statuta, vol. ii., p. 3, 1862). Attendance on the Anglican Chapel service and Communicating were of course intended as tests and pledges of Conformity.

[63] Parliamentary Debates.

[64] William Conyngham, Lord, and Lord Chancellor Plunket was the son of the Rev. Thomas Plunket, minister of the Strand-street Unitarian Congregation, who died on the 18th Sept., 1776. There is a very eulogistic notice of him in the *Freeman's Journal* of the date.

Trinity College, Dublin, is invested with a negative on the proceedings of the Senior Fellows by the Charter and Statutes of the College."

The pamphlet is traditionally ascribed to the Rev. G. Miller, F.T.C.D., who gave such important evidence before the parliamentary committee; and, substantially, it is based upon the arbitrary acts of the Provost, which were brought out before the committee, and which are more fully stated in the "Lachrymæ" and "Pranceriana."

The "Enquiry" asserts that the Provost claimed and exerted a negative upon all Board proceedings; and that in the election of Fellows and Scholars he had not only a negative but a final affirmative. The writer maintains that this, although the traditional, was not the true sense of the Statutes; and that by the Statutes the Provost had no greater power than the head of any other Corporation. He argues very closely and clearly to this purpose in regard of elections especially, from the grammatical meaning of *"unâ cum"* and *"cum;"* and he shows that what the Statute requires is merely the *presence* of the Provost, and that then, like the rest, he is bound by a majority decision. The writer is more subtle and less convincing in his solution of the last clause of the statute beginning *"Quod si primo."*[65]

Mr. Miller submitted a statement of the case for legal opinion, and obtained opinions supporting his own view from Sir William Scott (Lord Stowel), Sir Michael Smith, (Baron of the Exchequer and Master of the Rolls), Edward Law (Lord Ellenborough), Arthur Wolfe (Lord Kilwarden, Lord Chief Justice), and others.

The three questions were: (1) Had the Provost an absolute negative on Board Proceedings? (2) Was he concluded by the concurring votes of five Senior Fellows? (3) Could he nominate Fellows and Scholars to the exclusion of a candidate by a majority of the electors?

The first and third were answered in the negative; and the second in the affirmative by all the lawyers.[66]

While all these people were amusing themselves anatomising the Provost, he was not by any means silent on his own side. Besides his speeches in Parliament and his utterances at the Privy Council and at the Board, he had recourse to the public press. He sent a vindication of himself to the *Hibernian Journal*, which Duigenan says was the beginning of all the writing. The Provost also published by Leathley, Bookseller to the University, a pamphlet entitled, "Regulations made in Trinity College since the appointment of the Provost," and "Pranceriana" says that

---

[65] Down to the alterations made in the Statutes by the Queen's Letter of 1855, the words of the Lit. Pat. of Charles I. were:—*"in quem vel quos major pars Sociorum Seniorum unâ cum Præposito, vel eo absente, Vice Præposito consensisse deprehendetur, is, vel illi pro electo vel electis habeantur, et mox pronunciabuntur a Præposito. Quod si primo, vel Secundo Scrutinio electorum major pars, cum Præposito, vel eo absente, Vice Præposito non consenserint, eo casu in tertio Scrutinio, is, vel illi pro electo, vel electis sunto, quem, vel quos, Præpositus, vel eo absente Vice Præpositus, nominabit."* [Caput xxv. De Elect. form. et temp.]

[66] See also "An Enquiry how far the Provost of Trinity College is invested with a negative on the Proceedings of the Senior Fellows" (1790), by Dr. Young, Ex-Fellow and afterwards Bishop of Clonfert. It takes the same view of the case as that put forward in Miller's pamphlet.—[*Halliday Collection.*]

the unlucky pamphlet was withdrawn promptly after the attack made upon it in the *Hibernian*. It was for this attack that the Provost had the editor of the journal, Mr. James Mills, ducked under the College pump. This smashing article is No. 27 in the "Pranceriana Collection," and it certainly is a notable piece of criticism. It was attributed to the pen of Malone, the editor of "Shakespeare." It is, perhaps, worth mentioning here, that as the College Library was without a copy of the Provost's book until the year 1853, so it was without a copy of "Pranceriana" until the year 1880. *Trinitas incuriosa suorum!* The copy of the "Pranceriana" in the Library is the Second Edition, 1784, with the Appendix of 1776.

All the foregoing testimonies are damaging to the Provost's memory; but it is only fair to remember that all of them are the utterances of men who were his envious and unscrupulous personal enemies. In some respects John Hely Hutchinson was bad enough, but the most abiding charge against him is that of greediness and place-traffic; and in this transgression it is probable that he only sinned more deeply than most of the public men around him. He certainly was audacious in his demands, but he was a king in jobbery. What Duigenan does not at all account for is, how Hutchinson was able to drive all these flourishing bargains, and to hold such high place under various administrations and in the teeth of combining rivalries— and still this is a circumstance that ought, biographically, to be accounted for. The etiology is supplied in other contemporary sources, written in a more discerning spirit—and it is this, that the Provost was a man of immense ability, and of rare personal ascendency. He possessed, moreover, in a signal degree, the undaunted personal courage which, as mentioned further on,[67] was inherited by his sons and grandson; although Duigenan, who was himself very much of the Bob Acre type, refuses him even this credit, and mocks his sham duels.[68] He knew how to make himself both dreaded and desired by the Government, for he could be either its greatest help or its most formidable opponent. He knew the men he had to deal with, and he dealt with them according to the knowledge.

We have descriptions of the Provost in many contemporary works, and these descriptions, while they make no secret of his rapacity, present a strong reverse side to the "Pranceriana" picture.[69]

[67] Note A.

[68] Hutchinson had to say to three of these affairs of honour, and according to Duigenan he came badly out of all of them. Duigenan himself, it should be observed, once had a sham duel, in which he did not figure at all brilliantly, according to the orthodox interpretation of the code. He had insulted Sir Richard Borough so grossly that a meeting could not be evaded, and when the paces were measured Duigenan refused to take up the pistols, which in due form were laid at his feet. He then shouted to the "old rascal to fire away," and when Borough thereon left the field Duigenan declined to fight with his second, because he "had too great a regard for him to kill him."

[69] In George Faulkner's "Epistle to Howard" (1771), contained in the Halliday Collection in the Royal Irish Academy, we have—

> "Thou Hutchinson whom every muse
> With winning grace and art endues,
> Whose power 'gainst prejudice contends
> And proves that law and wit are friends—
> In that promiscuous page alone

Thus Hardy[70] says: "John Hely Hutchinson, father to the Earl of Donoughmore and Lord Hutchinson, introduced a classical idiom into the House of Commons. No member was ever more extolled than he was on his first appearance there. He opposed Government on almost every question, but his opposition was of no long continuance. As an orator his expression was fluent, easy, and lively; his wit fertile and abundant; his invective admirable, not so much from any particular energy of temperament or diction, as from being always unclogged with anything superfluous, or which could at all diminish the justness and brilliancy of its colouring. It ran along with the feelings of the House and never went beyond them.... The consequence of this assumed calmness was that he never was stopped.... The members for a long time remembered his satire, and the objects of it seldom forgave it.... In his personal contests with Mr. Flood (and in the more early part of their parliamentary careers they were engaged in many) he is supposed to have had the advantage.... To Flood's anger, Hutchinson opposed the powers of ridicule; to his strength he opposed refinement; to the weight of his oratory an easy, flexible ingenuity, nice discrimination, and graceful appeal to the passions. As the debate ran high, Flood's eloquence alternately displayed austere reasoning and tempestuous reproof; its colours were chaste but gloomy; Hutchinson's, on the contrary, were of 'those which April wears,' bright, various, and transitory; but it was a vernal evening after a storm, and he was esteemed the most successful because he was the most pleasing.... Mr. Gerrard Hamilton (than whom a better judge of public speaking has seldom been seen) observed that in his support of Government Hutchinson had always something to say which gratified the House. 'He can go out in all weathers, and as a debater is therefore inestimable.' He had attended much to the stage, and in his younger days he lived on great habits of intimacy with Quin, who admired his talents and improved his elocution.... He never recommended a bad measure, nor appeared a champion for British interest in preference to that of his own country. He was not awed into silence; he supported the Octennial Bill, the Free Trade Bill, and the Catholic Bill.... His acceptance of the Provostship of Trinity College was an unwise step.... After a long enjoyment of parliamentary fame it was then said that he was no speaker, and after the most lucrative practice at the Bar that he was no lawyer.... His country thought far otherwise, and his reputation as a man of genius, and an active, well-informed statesman, remained undiminished to the last. He left the opposition in 1760, and took the Prime Serjeancy.... In private life he was amiable, and in the several duties of father and husband most exemplary. In 1789, on the debate about the Prince of Wales's regency, Grattan opposing the administration was supported with great ability by Hutchinson, then Secretary of State. In the Lords, Lord Donoughmore took the same side. In 1792, in the debate on Langrishe's Bill for the restoration of the elective franchise to Irish Catholics, Hutchinson's two sons (Francis [?], afterwards Lord Donoughmore, and the one afterwards Lord Hutchinson) voted in the minority with the patriots."

The *Gentleman's Magazine* (1794) says that he was a wondrously gifted man and one of the most remarkable persons that this country ever produced. At the same time it calls him a rank courtier, and recites most of the "Pranceriana" and

---

By letters J. H. H. art known."
[70] ["Life of Lord Charlemont."]

"Lachrymæ" tattle against him.

Grattan and Grattan's son held a very high opinion both of his genius and of his fidelity to the interests of Ireland. Both of the Grattans, on the other hand, had a horror of Duigenan, as a truculent and coarse vulgarian. It is in Grattan's "Life" that we are told about Duigenan's threatening in the Law Courts to "bulge the Provost's eye," and it is there that Curran's epigram on Duigenan's oratory is preserved.[71]

Grattan says that Hutchinson supported every honest measure—all the main and essential ones, such as the Claim of Right, Free Trade, the Catholic Bills, Reform, and the Pension Bill. *"He was the servant of many governments, but he was an Irishman notwithstanding."* He possessed greater power of satire than any man of his day, and Grattan quotes Horace Walpole's anecdote about his habit of annoying Rigby and the Government when he wanted to make himself disagreeable to them. At other times he was immensely useful to the Government. Grattan considered that his chief fault was want of openness and directness of character, together with love of self-advancement. He was an enthusiastic admirer of Grattan, and took a prominent part in demanding for him the national presentation in 1782.

Taylor[72] says that Hutchinson was a very effective Provost, that he restored the discipline of the place, and that to him the University owes the improvement of the modern languages professorships. Taylor adds that he was a man of an enlightened mind and extended views, and that it is now admitted his views were consonant with the best principles of education.

Lord North knew Hutchinson's peculiarity well, and he said that "if England and Ireland were given to him he would want the Isle of Man for a potato garden." The Duke of Rutland, Lord Lieutenant here in 1784, formed a similar estimate, when he wrote that "the Provost had always some object in view, and that his objects were not generally marked with the character of moderation and humility."[73]

Dr. Wills[74] gives Provost Hely Hutchinson a very high place amongst the eminent men of the country, and mentions his eloquence and college reforms as well as his greed.

Even Mr. Froude,[75] who vastly dislikes himself and his sons, is constrained to call him the "able and brilliant Hely Hutchinson," and to tell of his "meridian splendour." He quotes Lord Lieutenant Townshend's statement that he was "the most popular man in parliament to conduct a debate."

The famous Colonel Isaac Barrè,[76] who, as he got Scholarship in 1744, was a college class-fellow of Hutchinson, gives the following description of him in 1768:—"When the Army Augmentation Bill was introduced by Tom Connoly, it

---

[71] See Note C.

[72] "History of the University of Dublin," p. 253, &c.

[73] "Froude," vol. ii. p. 104.

[74] "Distinguished Irishmen," vol. v. p. 233, &c.

[75] "English in Ireland," *passim.*

[76] Barrè was over here at that time as Vice-Treasurer, &c. He received the Freedom of Dublin in 1776.

was opposed by Sexten Pery on constitutional grounds, and by the Attorney General (Tisdall) on grounds that left him free to support the Bill afterwards if it were his interest to do so.[77]

"The Prime Serjeant (Hutchinson)" says Barrè "was not so prudent[78] (as Tisdall), and opposed it in a long, languid speech, full of false calculations; among the rest this curious one, that adding £40,000 per annum to the national expense was, in fact, adding a million to its debt, and that the nation, in the next session, would be £1,800,000 in debt. If all this is true, how will he have the impudence to support this measure hereafter? But, indeed, he has contradicted himself three or four times in the course of this session upon this subject.[79] He talks now of being dismissed. His profit by his employment is trifling, not above three or four hundred a year.[80]

[77] The Bill was to raise the army in Ireland to 15,500 men. Pery and the Nationalists saw that the object of the Crown was to have troops to send to America to crush the Colonists, and this they would not have on any terms. The Government, in reply, passed an Act through the English Parliament, giving satisfactory security that the full force of 12,000 should be kept in Ireland. Nationalists now have not to complain of any want of troops in this country, and we do not hear of their demanding any "satisfactory assurance" of the permanence of the forces.

Nothing could exceed the eagerness of the English Ministry to have the Army Augmentation Bill passed through the Irish Parliament. Lord Shelbourne, the English Home Secretary, wrote to Lord Lieutenant Townshend (March 1768) (*a*) that he would not hear of Malone's and Hutchinson's suggestions of delay in bringing in the Bill. He further announced that the English Parliament had passed an Act taking off the limitation of the troops in Ireland, imposed by the 10th of William III., and pledging that a full force of 12,000 men should be kept in Ireland. Sexten Pery led the opposition, which defeated the Bill by a majority of four. The Irish parliament was prorogued and dissolved, and did not meet for sixteen months, when they again threw out the Army Bill. Eventually, in November, 1769, Townshend succeeded in having the clause carried in another Act, whereby 3,235 men, in addition to the 12,000 to be kept here, were voted.

In 1775, Lord Lieutenant Harcourt asked for 4,000 men for the king out of the Irish establishment to be despatched to America, and he offered to supply their place by German Protestant troops. Anthony Malone was chairman of the Parliamentary Committee which, after a warm debate, granted the contingent as "armed negotiators," but rejected the Hessians. Grattan afterwards fiercely, and not unfairly, assailed Flood for carrying this discreditable measure. The troops were in time for the surrenders at Saratoga and Yorktown. Lord Edward Fitzgerald, one regrets to read, served on this expedition as aide-de-camp to Lord Moira. Lord Effingham, on the other hand, resigned his regiment rather than serve against those who were struggling for freedom, and he was twice publicly thanked by the people of Dublin. —[*Plowden* and *Mitchell*.]

In 1782, the king was allowed to draw 5,000 men out of the kingdom. In 1793, the Irish force was raised to 20,232. Most of these acts were for one year.

(*a*) "Life of Shelbourne," vol. ii., p. 12.

[78] In the debate (1772) on the Altered Money Bill, Hutchinson seems to have recovered his prudence.

[79] Another page shows how he was compensated for this "trifling profit" of the Prime Serjeancy.

[80] *Baratariana* says:—

"He is personally disliked, a mean gambler—not one great point in him—and exceedingly unpopular in this country. I must tell you a short anecdote which put him very much out of temper. The day after the first division he came to Council in a hackney chair, which happened, unluckily, to be No. 108 (the number of the majority). A young officer at the Castle wrote under the number of the chair, "COURT" in large characters, and at the top a coronet was drawn.[81]

"He denied positively in the beginning of his speech, any bargain or terms proposed by him at the Castle, but was not believed.... As far as I am able to judge," continues Barrè, "this country is manageable easily enough. The prevailing faction exists only by your want of system in England. They have no abilities, and their present and only friend, Hutchinson (for Tisdall is quite broken), cannot be depended on for a moment."

In the last volume (vol. viii.) of the "Historical Manuscripts Report" we find some very interesting mentions of Hutchinson in the letters that passed between "Single Speech" Hamilton and Edmund Sexten Pery. Both of these eminent men entertained a high opinion of, and a sincere personal regard for, the Provost. In 1771, Hamilton, who was Chancellor of the Irish Exchequer, and had been Chief Secretary to two Lord Lieutenants (Lords Halifax and Northumberland) wrote to Pery, the Speaker[82] of the House:—"As long as you and Andrews and Hutchinson are in being and business, Ireland will never want attractions sufficient to make me prefer it to a situation of 'more splendour and greater influence.'"

Two years later, Hamilton wrote to Pery about the collapse of the negotiations for his resigning the Exchequer Chancellorship in Hutchinson's favour, and begged that Hutchinson would not again require him to sacrifice his own solid and substantial interests. Another letter, dated 1779, says that Flood was eagerly canvassing for the post, and that Hutchinson was discontented. The Chancellorship was not given to either of the rivals—it was given to Foster, who was afterwards Speaker; and Hutchinson accordingly failed to score a second triumph over "the generous-minded, ornamental, sonorous-voiced Henry Flood, who was eclipsing his meridian splendour."[83]

In 1777 the Corporation of Dublin petitioned the Provost and Board for a free education for the son of the deceased patriot, Dr. Lucas. The College authorities responded in a literal spirit, and generously granted to the lad not only a remission

> "The Prime Serjeant, then, with a shuffling preamble
> Like a nag that before he can canter must amble,
> Betwixt right and wrong made a whimsical shamble,
> Which nobody can deny.
>
> 'Twas important, he said, and availed not a groat;
> But whether 'twas right or whether 'twas naught,
> Or whether he'd vote for it, or whether he'd not
> He'd neither assert nor deny."

[81] One of the rewards that Hutchinson demanded from the Government as the price of his support was, that his wife should be made a baroness. [Lord Lieutenant Townshend's letter, quoted by Froude, vol. ii., p. 67, and by Lord Fitzmaurice, vol. ii., p. 102.]

[82] See note E.

[83] *Froude*, vol. ii., p. 50.

of fees, but free rooms and free commons as well.[84]

In 1779, were published the "Commercial Restraints," which in its original shape was, a contribution to Lord Lieutenant Buckinghamshire as to the best method of extricating the country from its discontent and troubles. Froude says (vol. ii., p. 223), that it was the most important of all the opinions gathered by the Viceroy, and that it earned Hutchinson's pardon from Irish patriotism for his subserviency to the Court and Lord Townshend. The work is an extremely able review of the whole history and condition of our native Irish trade and industries, and it is as loyal in its nationality as it is able. It is the only specimen we have to show us the Provost as a writer and as an economist, and it certainly secures him a high place in these two estimates.

In this aspect the work possesses a great biographical value, inasmuch as it serves to complete the likeness of the Provost, and the complement which it supplies falls in line with the best features of the original. Although his sentences are often slovenly and sometimes ungrammatical, he could write forcibly and clearly, as well as speak persuasively and rhetorically; he could make facts and figures deliver their lesson; he could summon up the ghost of the past to illustrate and enforce the duties of the present; he could enwrap a message of peace in a mantle of warning; and when no selfish interest intervened he could fling his sword into the scale that was freighted with his country's welfare.

During Hutchinson's Provostship His Excellency the Lord Lieutenant, Lord Buckinghamshire, went in state to the University, and was received at the entrance of the Old Hall by the Provost and Fellows. At his entrance, Dr. Kearney made an eloquent oration; at the printing office, where H. E. was entertained with a view of the artists, another oration was delivered by Mr. Hutchinson, youngest (?) son of the Provost; at the Anatomy and Philosophical Rooms addresses were delivered by the Hon. Dr. Decourcy, son of Lord Kinsale, and the Hon. Mr. Jones, son of Lord Ranelagh. Thence he went to the Library, where an excellent oration was made by Dr. Leland, the Librarian, Orator, and Professor. H. E. afterwards dined in the New Hall with the Provost and Fellows, and numbers of the nobility and gentry. The elegance of the entertainment cannot be described, and is imagined to stand the College in no less than £700.[85]

In 1791 a Visitation by Lord Chancellor Lord Clare as Vice-Chancellor, and Dr. Fowler, Archbishop of Dublin, was held in the New Theatre, at the instance of the Provost, in reference to the complaint of Mr. Allen of having been unjustly kept out of Fellowship in 1790. The Visitors ruled that the question was not open to discussion, in consequence of the length of time which had elapsed. The Provost then brought forward his claim to the negative power over the proceedings of the Board, and was replied to by Drs. Kearney and Brown. The Provost argued from the Statutes and especially from the *Unâ cum Præposito* clauses, and spoke for three hours and a half with great ability. Mr. Miller spoke on behalf of the Junior

---

[84] [*Plowden.*] In 1736 the Board granted an allowance of £100 a year to Mr. Dunkin (who was Ball's predecessor in the Great Ship-street School), on Swift's appeal. —[*See Swift's Letters.*]

[85] Walk. *Hib. Mag.* 1777.

Fellows, touching their right to retain the emoluments of their pupils when they went out on livings. Miller was rebuked by the Chancellor for accusing the Provost of wanting to turn the disposal of pupils into a matter of patronage. The Rev. Mr. Burrowes and Mr. Magee spoke on the same side. Magee was personal, and on the Provost's protest the Chancellor stopped him. The Visitors declined to decide whether the Provost has an arbitrary election negative at the election of Fellows and Scholars; they ruled that the Provost has the power of disposing of pupils; and that he is bound by the majority of the Board. The Lord Chancellor bewailed the internal dissensions, alluded to his "own education in the College, and declared that there was not another University in Europe better calculated for the great purposes of promoting virtue and learning." The Visitation lasted three days.

In 1792, Hutchinson saw the Gardiner-Hobart Catholic Relief Bill carried, and three days after, the 26th of February, he saw the House of Parliament burned. On the 1st of March following Sir John Blacquiere repaid the University for its honorary degree by moving the thanks of the house to the College students for their spirited exertions in extinguishing the fire; and by suggesting that in acknowledgment of the daring bravery of the youths their old privilege of right of admission to the gallery should be restored to them. Mr. Hutchinson, the Member for the University, acknowledged the compliment with becoming pride and dignity. The Provost's last reported appearance in parliament was on the 6th of July, 1793, when he spoke in support of the Bill for the Charitable Musical Society. In the previous month, on one of the Militia Bills, he defended his son Francis from a rebuke of Mr. Secretary Hobart, though he voted against the son.

In that his last session, he saw carried — and along with Grattan, Forbes, Yelverton, Gardiner, and the other Liberals helped to carry — the Place, Pensions, Barren Land, and India Trade Acts. He introduced the bills for the Parliament grant of £1,300[86] to establish the College Botanical Gardens, and he earnestly supported Knox's Bill for admitting Catholics to Parliament.

He presided at the Board of Trinity College for the last time on the 25th of August this same year. His health was giving way, and his old enemy, the gout, was prevailing against him.

In the political side of his career Hutchinson saw a wondrous change in the meaning and method of Irish parliamentary life. When he began (1759) to take part in public affairs, the Irish parliament was at about its lowest level of degradation. Having been abolished by Cromwell and re-created by Charles II., it had become from the time of the Restoration little else than an office for registering and levying the English orders for pensions and salaries, and for passing the Money Bills. Poyning's Act and the 6th of George I. were in such active operation that the Government asserted the power of originating and altering the Money Bills, and that Anthony Malone was dismissed first from the Prime Serjeancy and later from the Exchequer Chancellorship for denying his right. A few years later, Lord Lieutenant Townshend, came over here for the express purpose of smashing the Irish Junto, and he smashed it by the simple process of taking the bribery into his own

---

[86] Walk. *Hib. Mag.* 1791.

hands,[87] and making it, what Sir Arthur Wellesley[88] forty years after found it, an English state department.[89] He was so indignant with the Commons for rejecting an altered Money Bill that he entered a protest on the Lords' Journal and prorogued the Parliament.[90] Down to Hutchinson's time the Lord Lieutenants were absentees, and the Lords Justices were the centre of the Junto of "Undertakers" who undertook to the English Government to manage business here—i.e. "their own business"—on their own conditions. In the National Senate there was no national or intellectual life, and scarcely a name has survived in history.

There are no Reports of debates until the year 1781; for over 50 years scarcely a single important measure was passed;[91] place holders in parliament were multiplied, and the pension and salary lists increased in proportion.[92] To lessen the

[87] In 1771, John Ponsonby resigned the Speakership rather than present to Lord Townshend the adulatory Address of the House of Commons, and Pery was, by Government influence, elected in his room.

[88] See Wellington's Correspondence.

[89] Grattan said Townsend was a corrupter, and Buckingham a jobber in a mask.

[90] On this prorogation, "Baratariana" has—

> "Our worthy Lieutenant comes down to the House,
> Protests their proceedings are not worth a louse,
> And leaving undone the affairs of the nation,
> The session concludes with a d——d prorogation,
> Derry down.
>
> "Here mark, my dear friends, that our ruin's completed
> Since a parliament's useless which thus can be treated;
> While they served his foul purpose he'll fawn and collogue them,
> But if once they do right he'll that instant prorogue them.
> Derry down."

[91] In 1739 the English parliament passed an Act removing the duties on some of the Irish Woollen Exports, and this was done for the benefit of the English wool manufacturers.

[92] Out of 300 members 104 held places, and 120 were nominated by patrons under the influence of Government. The civil establishment, with its contingent expenses, amounted to over half a million sterling a year, while the entire revenue of the kingdom was under a million and a quarter.—[*Pery.*] In 1789, Lord Jocelyn presented to the House, by order, the list of pensions. The civil pensions amounted to £97,850, and the military pensions to £5,827.

In Grattan's Life, vol. iv., p. 14, the placemen in parliament are enumerated, and the list shows:—

In the military department	36
In the law department	38
In the revenue department	38
In state and miscellaneous department	9
Pensions	7
Total	109

Lib. Mun. vol. i. part 1, enumerates 389 patent offices in the establishment of Ireland—amongst them are: Keeper of the Signet, Under Secretary of State for the Civil Department, do. for Military Do., Pursuivant, Master of the Game, Interpreter of Irish tongue, Star Chamber, with Commissioners, Marshals, clerks, &c., Courts of Wards and Liveries

balance available for this bribery, the surplus revenue was expended in local and private jobs.[93] The Mutiny Act was perpetual; parliaments ran for the monarch's life, judges held at pleasure, Catholics were debarred the franchise and education; Anglican State Protestantism was built up by cruelty and crime, complaints of grievances were met by commendations of the Charter Schools, and the trade and industries of the country were suffered, without remonstrance, to lie strangled under the jealous and grasping commercial restraints imposed by the English Parliament.

All these things Hely Hutchinson saw when he first looked out on the field of Irish administration; and before he died he saw most of these reproaches swept away by the operation of the courage, and intellect, and vigour which, contemporaneously with himself, found their way into the Commons House. Sexten Pery was a few years before him, and "Sexten Pery," says Grattan, "was the original fountain of all the good that befell Ireland." Flood entered parliament the same year as Hutchinson, Hussey Burgh, and Gardiner a few years later, and then came Yelverton and Grattan, and by the power of these resolute anti-Englishers the face of the country was changed. They found Ireland a child, and they watched her growth from infancy to arms, and from arms to liberty. They led the Volunteers to victory, and wrung back a portion of the people's rights from the frightened oppressor.[94]

---

with Masters; fœdaries, &c., the Court of Palatines, the Lord Almoner, the Vice-Treasurer, Transcriptor and Foreign Apposer, Summonister and Clerk of Estreats, the Trustees of the Linen Manufacture, Commissioners of Wide Streets, Commissioners of Array, Constables of Castles, Muster Master General, Commissioners for Victualling, Provincial Provost Martials, Alnager, Clerk of the Pells, Vice-treasurer, Clerk of the Lords, Clerk of the Commons, six Clerks of Chancery, Principal Secretaries of State, Prime Serjeant, Lord High Treasurer, Chancellor of the Exchequer, Auditor-General, Commissioners of Treasury, Commissioners of Accounts, First Clerk, Second and Third Clerk to do.; Commissioner of Appeals, Commissioners of Stamps, Hearth Money Collectors, Poll Tax Collectors, Cursitors in Chancery, Register of Appeals Spiritual, Clerk of the Pipe, Prothonotary, Philizer, or Filacer Clerk of Privy Council, Wine-taster, Escheator, Searcher, Packers, Craners, Seneschals, Presidents of the Four Provinces, Governors of Forts, Clerks of the First Fruits, Deputy Master of the Rolls, Examinators, Master of the Revels, Clerk of the Nickells, Exigenter, Clerk of the Outlawries, Clerk of the Essions, Chirographers, Sirographers, &c., &c.

[93] The first real and important debate in the Irish Parliament was in 1753, on the Money Bill, on the Commons' power to dispose of surplus revenue.

The beginning of useful practical legislation for the country was made in 1757 by Edmund Sexten Pery's Land Carriage Act, giving bounties on the land carriage of corn to Dublin. In the same year he carried another Act giving bounties on ship carriage of coal to Dublin.

[94] In the single year of 1782 (short parliaments and free trade having been already secured)—

> The Bank of Ireland was established.
> Habeas Corpus was made law.
> The Sacramental test for Protestant nonconformists was abolished.
> Poyning's Act and 6th of George I. were repealed.
> The perpetual Mutiny Act was repealed.
> Judges appointed *quam diu*.

To this change Hutchinson directly, and still more indirectly, contributed. He quickened the parliamentary tone, and lifted its level. He was the father of the cultivated style of oratory which henceforward characterised the debates; he was the best debater in the house, and, after Grattan, the finest speaker. He could patriotise, and he could philippise; and whether he patriotised or philippised, he did it formidably and efficiently. He was venal, but he feared no man's face; he was a ready-money voter, but he could go out in all weathers. He trafficked, without satiety, in patents and sinecures for himself and his sons, but he insisted on Free Trade for Ireland.[95]

Take him for all in all, and the first John Hely Hutchinson certainly presents a very rare combination of striking features. He was a representative man of a remarkable age, and he sprung out of the conditions of a period which he very much helped to mould. He was endowed with leading abilities, and was disfigured by hideous blemishes. From an humble start in life he made his way to the high places of the field, and, without any surroundings, he raised himself to be a living power in the State. He was mighty in speech, in courage, in council, and in achievement; and he could be craven, vindictive, corrupting, and paltry. In invective he was unequalled; and he was more sorely scorched by ridicule and rebuke than any man of his day. He lived in perpetual discords and in endless schemes, and the success which, in the main, followed him was chequered by bitter defeats and mortifications. He enjoyed a splendid fortune, maintained a lordly style, and wielded vast influence, and not a single generous action is recorded of him. Negligent of learning, he became the head of the University in one of its periods of peculiar brilliancy, and, having for twenty years drawn its revenues and exploited its resources, he is not named in its list of benefactors. He reared a numerous, affectionate, gifted, and successful family, and he founded a peerage.[96]

However unprincipled Hutchinson was in his bargainings with the Castle, he <u>was often sound and straight on national and Catholic questions</u>. He was an en-
    A great Catholic Relief Act, including education, was carried.
    Parliamentary independence was achieved.

Grattan's parliament did not keep up to this high level of public spirit. It sank and perished by its own unreformed corruption.

[95] "Free Trade for Ireland," in 1779, meant something quite distinct from the political economy free trade of the present day. The latter means an exemption from all duties to the State on exports and imports; whereas the former meant a release from the restrictions on Irish trade imposed by England for the benefit of England. The reform of 1779 continued the duties, but enjoined that they should be imposed by the native parliament for the benefit of the Irish kingdom. The Irish Free Trade Parliament was Protectionist. In the November of 1779 Grattan's amendment on the Address, supported by Hussey Burgh and the volunteers, demanding Free Trade, was carried. In February 1780 the concession was made by England, and the Provost's book had a large share in the triumph. — [See Mitchel.]

It was on the debate on the Short Supply in connection with this measure that Hussey Burgh said, and lost the Prime Serjeancy for saying, "The English have sowed their laws like serpents' teeth and they have sprung up in armed men."

[96] One other provost, Archbishop Loftus; one chancellor, Lord Cairns; two vice-chancellors, Bishop Jones and John Fitzgibbon; one fellow, Bishop Howard; and three scholars, Yelverton, Wolfe, and Plunket, also founded noble houses.

thusiastic admirer of Grattan, and, on essential matters touching the interests and dignity of the country, he gave Grattan a cordial and effective support. The proudest passage in his life was the day (16th April, 1782) when, as Principal Secretary of State, he read out to the Irish Parliament the king's message, practically conceding independence.[97] There is not in Anglo-Irish history another event of equal grandeur; and Hely Hutchinson's Provostship for ever and inseparably connects the College with the climax of a triumph over English arrogance and obstinacy which, in the main, was won by a phalanx of her own sons when the prince of all the land led them on.[98]

*   *   *   *   *

The Will of "John Hely Hutchinson, His Majesty's Principal Secretary of State," made in 1788—proved and probate granted in November, 1794, by the Right Worshipful Patrick Duigenan, Doctor of Laws, Commissary, and so forth, is in the Public Record Office.

There are seven codicils of various dates, down to the year of the Provost's death. He says that no man ever had better or more dutiful and affectionate children—God bless them all—and amongst them he left £5,000 to each of his two eldest daughters, with 5 per cent. interest, and £4,000 to each of the two younger. He left £5,000 to his son Francis, as engaged at the time of his marriage, and to his sons John, Abraham, Christopher, and Lorenzo £4,000 each; £500 to Jane, eldest daughter of his worthy friend, Dr. Wilson. If any children should die before 21, or marriage, their share was to go amongst the younger children, but so as no younger child was to have more than £5,000 on the whole. All his real and personal estate,[99] subject to the foregoing legacies, he left to his dearly-beloved son, Lord Donoughmore, his sole executor. He was to raise the portions of the two younger daughters to £5,000, if the estate could afford it. His office in the Port of Strangford he considered part of his personal estate, having purchased it with the knowledge and at the desire of the Irish Government;[100] and he included it in the bequest to Lord Donoughmore for the lives in being. In a codicil (1789) he bequeathed £200 each to John, and to Abraham and Christopher while they shall continue at the Temple. Later codicils mention that some of these sums had been paid in full, and the legacies were accordingly revoked. He left his books on Morality, Divinity, and Poetry to Abraham, the law books to Francis, and the rest of his books to John. In a codicil of 1794, he left to Abraham "whose health is delicate," £100 a year till he shall obtain a net income of £200 yearly by some ecclesiastical preferment, this being in addition to the former legacy.[101] To his butler he left £20 a year, and to

---

[97] See the summary of his speech in Plowden.

[98] See Note D.

[99] It is not said what either the real or the personal estate amounted to. In De Burgh's "Landowners of Ireland," the Donoughmore property is set down at 11,950 acres, with the Government valuation of £10,466. The Tipperary portion is 4,711 acres, and £4,764. The other portions are situate in Galway, Cork, Dublin, Kilkenny, Louth, Monahan, Waterford, and Wexford.

[100] He does not say what price he paid for it, or from whom he purchased it. Probably it was part of his place-traffic with Blaquiere.

[101] Doubtless this is the "A. Hely Hutchinson" whose autograph appears in the

another servant £20. He desired his manuscript essay towards a history of the College[102] to be published, being first perused by his son, Lord Donoughmore.[103] He directed his body to be opened, and to be laid by his late dear wife.

*   *   *   *   *

The following Will which laid the foundation of the fortunes of the family is also in the Public Record Office:—

"The last Will and Testament of Richard Hutchinson of Knocklofty, in the county of Tipperary, Esq. Whereas I have this day executed a deed, whereby it appears that there are several sums now affecting my estate, and amounting in the whole to the sum of ten thousand nine hundred and fifty-two pounds four shillings and a farthing; and whereas Ann Mauzy, widow, and Lewis Mauzy, her son, have agreed to accept the sum of four thousand pounds in lieu of all their claims and demands. Now it is my will that such personal fortune as I now, or at the time of my death shall be possessed of shall be applied, in the first place, towards paying and discharging such sums of money as John Hely Hutchinson, Esq., shall think proper to pay the said Ann Mauzy, provided the same does not exceed the said sum of four thousand pounds; and the rest and residue of my personal estate and fortune if anything shall remain, I bequeath to my beloved niece, Christian Hely Hutchinson.

"Witness my hand and seal, this fourth day of August, one thousand seven hundred and fifty-seven.

"RICHARD HUTCHINSON."

Preacher's Book of S. Bride's, Dublin, in the year 1796. Under the autograph there is written, in a different hand and in different ink, "Now an officer in H.M.'s Service."

[102] This is the only mention of the College; in the Will. The Provost left it no bequest, and did not even designate himself as Provost.

[103] This direction has never been carried out. The MS. is known to be in existence; and would it not be seemly and desirable to have it deposited in the College Manuscript Room?

NOTES.

NOTE A. PAGE X.
THE HUTCHINSON FAMILY.

The Provost left six sons and four daughters. Five of the sons took degrees in the University, viz.:—

Richard Hely—on an Oxford Ad Eundem—B.A. 1775, M.A. 1780, LL.B. and LL.D. 1780.

Francis Hely—B.A. 1779, M.A. 1783.

Christopher Hely—B.A. 1788.

Abraham Hely—B.A. 1788, M.A. 1791; and Lorenzo Hely—B.A. 1790.

RICHARD HELY, the eldest son, and the first Lord Donoughmore, was a Commissioner of Accounts, Second Remembrancer, Chief Commissioner of Excise, Commissioner of Customs, Commissioner of Stamps, and Postmaster-General.

In 1776, he was elected simultaneously representative for Sligo and for the University (against the Attorney-General, Philip Tisdall), and chose the latter. He was unseated by parliamentary committee as not duly elected; and, in 1777, he was re-elected for Sligo without a new writ. In the University he was replaced by John Fitzgibbon (Earl of Clare). In 1783 he was M.P. for Taghmon. In 1788, he succeeded to the title, on the death of his mother, and served in the Upper House, while his father and his two brothers were in the Commons. In 1794, according to the custom of the times, he raised a regiment, and got the command of it for his celebrated brother John.

FRANCIS HELY was returned for the University in the election of 1790. In the following year took place the celebrated petition against his return, which is related in page xxvii, &c. In 1799, he was member for Naas, and was re-elected in 1800, on having been appointed to the office of collector for the Port of Dublin. In 1792, on the debate on receiving the Catholic petition in connection with Langrishe's Bill for giving, or giving back, the franchise, &c., to the Catholics, Mr. Froude says that: "Francis Hutchinson, the Provost's second son, soared into nationalist rhetoric. 'When the pride of Britain was humbled in the dust,' he said, 'her enemies led captive the brightest jewel of the imperial crown torn from her diadem, at the moment when the combined fleets of the two great Catholic powers of Europe threatened a descent upon our coasts, from whom did we derive our protection then?'... 'We found it in the support of three millions of our fellow-citizens, in the spirit of our national character—in the virtue of our Catholic brethren.' The motion for the petition was lost by 208 votes to 23, and Langrishe's Bill was carried." —[*English in Ireland*, vol. iii., p. 53.]

Sir Jonah Barrington, in his "Personal Sketches." tells of the duel which Francis had at Donnybrook with Lord Mountmorris in 1798, in which his lordship was wounded.

CHRISTOPHER HELY was called to the Bar, but never much relished the profession, being altogether of a military turn. In 1795 he was elected member for Taghmon, county Wexford, in the Irish parliament on his father's death; and after the Union he represented Cork city in the Imperial parliament. He was Escheator of the Province of Munster. He was an earnest champion of the Catholic claims, as were also his father and brothers; he was a thorough supporter of the liberal policy of Lord Lieutenant Fitzwilliam; he mistrusted Lord Lieutenant Camden and Pitt, and he opposed the Union scheme. He is, however, far more celebrated as a soldier than as a lawyer or politician, and in 1796 he resigned his seat. He adored his brother John, rivalled his brilliant courage, and served under him and with him at home and abroad with great distinction. He joined him in Ireland as a volunteer on the breaking out of the disturbances in 1798; but both of the brothers speedily got disgusted with the odious work, as did Cornwallis, and Moore, and Abercrombie, and Lake, and every other high-minded soldier, including Colin Campbell, afterwards in the tithe war. John soon got ordered off to Flanders, under Abercrombie, to fight the French; and thither Christopher followed him, and was wounded at the battle of Alkmar. Christopher followed John also to Egypt, and afterwards on his mission to St. Petersburgh, and to Berlin. Christopher, on his own account, fought in the Russian ranks against the French, and was badly wounded by Benningsen's side at the battle of Eylau, in 1807. He fought also at the battle of Friedland. He died at Hampsted in 1825—[*Suppl. Biog. Univer.*] It is worth noticing that this invaluable biographical dictionary makes a mistake in regard of the Castlebar battle in 1798, and a mistake of a kind that is not usual in French historians in affairs that concern the military glory of France. At Castlebar the French were victorious, and the Hutchinsons and the English troops were defeated disgracefully. The *Biog. Univer.*, however, under *"Christophe Elie Hutchinson Cinquième fils de Jean Elie Hutchinson, Prevot de l'Universite de Dublin,"* says: *"Il eut part a l'affaire de Castlebar et fit prisonniers les deux Generaux Francais Lafontaine et Sorrazin au moment ou environnè par leur corps il se croyait et devoit se croire perdu, et s'acquit ainsi l'estime de General en Chef Lord Cornwallis."* The writer confounds Castlebar with Ballinamuck.

ABRAHAM HELY was Commissioner of Customs, and Port duties, according to the Lib. Mun. and Sir Bernard Burke; and a clergyman, according to his father's will.

Lorenzo Hely took Holy Orders.

Besides these five the Provost had a son—his second born—

JOHN HELY HUTCHINSON, the most distinguished of all. He was born in 1757, and entered the army in 1774, the year in which his father was made Provost. In 1789 he became M.P. for Taghmon, county Wexford, on his brother Richard's call to the upper house, and in 1790 he became member for Cork city (the father going to Taghmon), and continued so until the Union. In 1792, in the debate on receiving the Catholic Petition, "Prominent amongst their (Catholic) champions was Colonel Hutchinson, the Provost's son, who inherited his father's eloquence without his shrewdness. He talked the Liberal cant of the day, which may be compared instructively with the modern Papal syllabus." — [*Froude*, vol. iii., p. 53.]

Mr. Froude cannot have read this speech. It is a fervid denunciation of the penal laws, and of their cruelties and mischief; and it does not "talk either Liberal cant or Papal syllabus." Colonel Hutchinson's two speeches on the Petition and on Langrishe's Bill, even as summarised in the Irish Parliamentary Report, are enlightened, able, and eloquent oratory. He was for complete emancipation. His liberal address to the Cork constituency, in 1796, is given by Plowden.

Hutchinson was an enthusiastic admirer of Lafayette, and of his ardent principles of popular liberty. When in Paris he attached himself closely to the general, and served on his personal staff.

During the troubles of 1798 he was employed here at the head of his brother's regiment, under Abercrombie. He sat in the Irish parliament in 1800, and voted for the Union! — [*Webb, and Barrington's "Black List."*]

He commanded against the French at Castlebar, and he shared in the humiliating defeat which Humbert's handful of men, supported by a body of Irish peasantry, inflicted on the royal army. Hutchinson was unable to stay the panic. His troops, which had signalised and enervated themselves by their licentious brutalities on a defenceless population, broke and fled — as Abercrombie foretold they would do — before the enemy. Their rout was as complete as it was disgraceful, and the barbarities which they committed on their retreat were diabolical. Hutchinson afterwards had the satisfaction of taking part in the affair at Ballinamuck, county Longford, where the French, including Generals Humbert, Sorrazin, and La Fontaine, laid down their arms. — [*Cornwallis's Correspondence*, vol. ii., p. 396; *Knight's History of England*, vol. vii., p. 367; *Haverty's History of Ireland*, p. 760; *and Bishop Stock's Narrative of Killala.*]

Hutchinson left the sickening Irish scenes, along with Abercrombie, for Flanders, in the Duke of York's expedition. After that he accompanied Abercrombie to Egypt as second in command, and on his death at Aboukir he succeeded as chief. He was reinforced from home, and by Sir David Baird's expeditionary contingent from India, took Alexandria and Cairo, and drove Menou and the French out of Egypt. For these distinguished achievements he was created Lord Hutchinson of Alexandria and Knocklofty; and, notwithstanding these achievements, he was never again employed in war service by the English Government. He made no secret of his anti-Toryism, and this was enough to ensure his rejection by a Government that selected the Chathams and Burrards. Lord Hutchinson was afterwards employed on some high diplomatic commissions at St. Petersburg and Berlin, and in these his independence of judgment was not altogether palatable to the London authorities. In 1825, on the death of his eldest brother, he succeeded to the Donoughmore title and estates, which, on his death without issue, in 1832, passed to his nephew, the third peer, better known as "Lavalette Hutchinson."

This JOHN HELY HUTCHINSON, the third of the name, was born in Wexford, in 1788. Having served through the Waterloo campaign, he was, on the allied occupation of Paris, in 1815, quartered there as Captain of the First Regiment of Grenadiers of the Guards. While there, in 1816, he, together with Lieutenant Bruce of his own regiment, and the celebrated Sir R. Wilson, effected Lavalette's escape from France, after his deliverance from the Conciergerie by the romantic devotion and bravery of his wife.

The three friends were prosecuted in Paris for this violation of the law. They declined to insist on their right of having half the jury English, and trusted themselves entirely to the honour of the Frenchmen. They admitted what was charged against them, and were condemned in the mild sentence of three months' imprisonment, and the costs of the prosecution. Captain Hutchinson, on the trial, told how he had lodged Lavalette in his own chambers for one night, supplied him with an English officer's costume from a Paris tailor, procured passes, and on horseback escorted to the frontier Lavalette, who was in a carriage with Wilson. He was willing to give a distinct answer to any fair question about himself, but he peremptorily refused to say anything that would compromise anyone else. He declared that there was not a particle of political animus in the adventure. The French historians tell how the chivalrous young Irishman's exploit was applauded by the whole nation, and how, on the trial, his manly and gracious bearing captured the court, which had to find him guilty of the deed that he acknowledged and related. Sir R. Wilson had been aide-de-camp to Hutchinson's uncle the general. [*Biog. des Contemp. and The Accusation, Examination, and Trial of Wilson, Hutchinson, and Bruce.*]

Captain Hutchinson succeeded to the title in 1832. He lived and died at Palmerston, and in Chapelizod church a memorial tablet is erected to him, with the following inscription:—"Sacred to the memory of John Hely Hutchinson, third Earl of Donoughmore, Knight of St. Patrick, Lord Lieutenant of the county of Tipperary, and a Privy Councillor, having served his country in the Peninsular War and the Senate; and his country in troublous times. He died on the 12th of September, 1851, in the 64th year of his age, loved, respected, and regretted by all who knew him. This tablet has been erected in the church where he usually worshipped to record his many virtues by his widow."

In Chapelizod churchyard there is a tombstone inscribed: "Beneath this stone rest the earthly remains of Mrs. Hely Hutchinson; departed this life 1st June, 1830, aged 72 years.

Between the Provost and his four sons they represented, for over 40 years, 11 constituencies, and besides this, one was in the Irish and English, and another in the English House of Lords.

The names of the Provost and of his son Richard are on the roll of the Irish M.P.'s (1783-90) which Dr. Ingram has had framed and hung up in the Fagel wing of the College Library.

The present Lord Donoughmore, who is sixth in descent from the Provost, was one of the European Commission for organising Eastern Roumelia under the

Berlin Treaty, and he is also the originator of the Lords' Committee of inquiry on the Irish Land Act. His lordship's father, in 1854, moved the second reading of Lord Dufferin's Liberal "Leasing Powers, and Landlord and Tenant Bills;" and in 1865 he made an able speech in the House of Lords on the grievances of the officers of the East India Company's army. He had previously served as a soldier with distinction in the East, and was always listened to with deserved attention by the peers. — [*Lord Dufferin's Speeches and Addresses.*]

NOTE B. PAGE XVII.

DR. LELAND.

Duigenan's disparaging mention of Dr. Leland is one of the most spiteful and unjust of his utterances. There does not seem to be any proof that Leland was guilty of any Academic disloyalty in being or becoming friendly to the Provost, and outside this indictment the celebrity of his varied intellectual distinctions added greatly to the lustre and dignity of the College. He was probably the best classical scholar of the country; he was an eloquent and popular preacher, constantly advocating the charities of the city, and although he did not contribute to either *Baratariana* or *Pranceriana* he was the most learned Irish author of the period. Dr. Thomas Leland was born in Dublin in 1722, and was educated in Sheridan's famous school in Capel-street. He entered College in 1737, got Scholarship in 1741, and Fellowship in 1746. In 1746 he was appointed Southwell lecturer in St. Werburgh's Church. He was Erasmus Smith Professor of Oratory and Modern History in the University, Librarian, Chaplain to Lord Lieutenant Townshend, Prebendary of St. Patrick's Cathedral, and Rector of Rathmichael, which living he exchanged for St. Anne's, Dublin, with the Vicar, Dr. Benjamin Domville Barrington. In 1781 he resigned his Senior Fellowship and retired on Ardstraw, which he held by dispensation along with St. Anne's until his death, in 1785. He was a vehement opposer of pluralists until he became himself a pluralist. He published a "Translation of Demosthenes," "The History of Philip of Macedon," and "The History of Ireland" in three volumes, quarto. This last-named history is really a work of very superior merit. Leland supported the English in the spirit of Primate Boulter; and like Delany, he may have hunted for a bishopric from the English Government; but as a historian, he gave an honest and able record. No one need set out more fairly and forcibly the rapacity of our Irish Reformationists, the frauds of Strafford, and the barbarities of Cromwell. His book was furthermore quite a novelty in regard of fresh material, and would be almost worth re-editing. After Leland's death three volumes of his sermons were published, by subscription, by M'Kenzie of Dame-street, and the list of subscribers contains the names of Provost Hutchinson, the Vice-Provost, many of the Fellows, the Library, bishops, judges, peers, members of parliament, and most of the celebrities of the day, but it does not contain the name of Patrick Duigenan.

Concerning the "History of Ireland," Leland's greatest work, we see by the recently-issued Historical Manuscripts Commission Report, that it was Charles O'Connor of Belanagare, the then most capable recordist of Ireland, who moved him (1767) to undertake it "because he has abilities and philosophy equal to the task." O'Connor writes again, that "we undoubtedly have [in Trinity College Library], by Dr. Leland's care, the best collection of old annals now in these islands. That learned and worthy gentleman has made me free of the College Library." In another letter O'Connor says: "Dr. Leland is now librarian, and promises me a warm room and all the liberty I can require relative to the College MSS., which are now a noble collection, indeed." It was Charles O'Connor who made Lord Lyttleton and Dr. Leland acquainted with each other, and we do not find it recorded that the English peer was of any service to the Irish scholar, although Dr. Leland generously supplied his lordship with valuable historical information for his history of Henry II.; and that, when he himself was engaged in describing the same events in his own work.—[See *Life* prefixed to Sermons, and vol. viii. of *Hist. Man. Com. Reports*, 1881, p. 486.]

Dr. Johnston had a high regard for Dr. Leland, and he wrote to him a letter of personal thanks for the Dublin University's honorary LL.D. in 1765. Johnston complained to O'Connor that Leland "begins his history too late," and that he should have been more exact in regard of "the times, for such there were, when Ireland was the school of the West, the quiet habitation of sanctity and literature." It was the chance mention of Leland's history that drew from Johnston the indignant exclamation "The Irish are in a most unnatural state, for we see there the minority prevailing over the majority. There is no instance, even in the ten persecutions, of such severity as that which the Protestants of Ireland have exercised against the Catholics." —[*Boswell.*]

In the *Anthologia Hibernica* for March, 1793, vol. i., p. 165, there is a notice of Leland which sharply disparages his "History of Ireland." The notice is otherwise friendly and appreciative, and it quotes Dr. Parr's eulogy on Dr. Leland.

His "History of Ireland" closes with the surrender of Limerick in 1691, and Hutchinson was correct in stating ("Letter 3," p. 11, *ante*) that Ireland had no professed historian of its own since that era, and that history furnished very imperfect and often partial views of her affairs.

NOTE C. PAGE XVII.

DR. DUIGENAN.

DR. PATRICK DUIGENAN, more familiarly termed "Paddy," was one of the most remarkable men enumerated in the list of the Fellows of Trinity College. He was the son of the Master of St. Bride's Parish School, and, doubtless, he received his early education in the school which, in his father's days, was kept first in Golden-lane and afterwards in Little Ship-street. In allusion to this, Watty Coxe's Journal twits him with the diploma of "St. Bride's College." From St. Bride's Parish School the lad Patrick was sent to St. Patrick's Cathedral School, then presided over by Mr. Sheills (or Shiel), and thence in the year 1753 he entered Trinity College, as a Sizar. Whether he obtained the Sizarship by competition or by nomination we do not find recorded; but *quocunque modo* a sizar he entered, and next to him on the form sat another sizar stripling, Barry Yelverton, afterwards an usher in Buck's School in North King-street, and subsequently Lord Chief Baron and Lord Avonmore.[104] In 1756, Duigenan obtained Scholarship; in 1761, Fellowship; and in 1776, he retired on the Professorship of Laws, having been, in fact, turned out by Provost Hutchinson. He was M.P. for Armagh, King's Advocate-General, Privy Councillor, Vicar-General, and Judge of the Prerogative Court. He was a blustering and honest man; a fanatical anti-Catholic and a fierce Unionist, and he is accordingly hero-worshipped by Mr. Froude. He was a hanger-on, first of Philip Tisdall, and then of Lord Clare.

Wills, in his "Distinguished Irishmen," says that Duigenan was the son of the parish clerk of St. Werburgh's; and Dr. Madden, in his "United Irishmen," gives a letter saying the same, and that the father died a Catholic. There is no foundation for either of these assertions. Hugh Duigenan, the father, died St. Bride's parish schoolmaster, and he, as well as his wife Priscilla, was buried in St. Bride's church-yard. It is said in the "Life of Curran" that Duigenan once avowed in the House of Commons that he was the son of a parish clerk, and if so the father must have held that office in Derry before he came to Dublin. Dr. Maddens contributor says that Duigenan was appointed to St. Bride's School through the influence of Fitz-gibbon, the father of Lord Clare. This is quite probable, as the Fitzgibbons lived in the parish—in Stephen-street, and many of the family were baptised in the church and buried in the graveyard. There may be truth in the tradition that the father was originally a Catholic and conformed. Grattan says that Duigenan was edu-cated for the Roman Catholic priesthood; that he was a hanger-on of Tisdall: that his manner of speaking resembled that of a mob-man in the last stage of agony; and Curran said his *"oratory was like the unrolling of a mummy, nothing but old bones and rotten rags,"* and that he had a vicious way of "gnawing the names of papists." He was employed by Castlereagh to administer the Union bribe of a million and a half, and in 1807 he was employed by Sir Arthur Wellesley, then Chief Secretary, to negotiate about the Charter Schools and the Irish Protestant bishops.[105] He was also one of the Public Record Commissioners.

His first wife was a Miss Cusack, a Catholic, and to her, in regard of religious matters he was most indulgent. This was the only instance of toleration that Dui-genan was ever known to show. In 1799 he supported Toler's (Lord Norbury) In-

[104] Duigenan's matriculation is—

> 1753—June. Patricius Duigenan, Siz., Filius Annum agens 16. Educa-tus sub ferula Mr. Sheill. Natus in Comtu Derri.

Dr. Lawson.

It would be a pity not to give the matriculation above his—

> "Barry Yelverton, Siz. Filius Franc. Gen. Annum agens 17. Educatus sub. fer. Mr. Egan. Natus in Comtu Cork.

Mr. Radcliffe."

These two poor Sizar boys, one from the North and the other from the South—meeting probably for the first time in the College hall and sitting side by side—what careers the Col-lege opened to them! Probably, there is not in all the matriculation books a more interesting page than the page which contains these two consecutive entries.

[105] "Wellington Correspondence."

demnity Bill, freeing all who in 1798 had committed illegal acts against the people. It must have cost him some trouble of mind when, as Vicar-General in 1783, he had to license Dr. Betagh's Catholic School in Fishamble-street, as well as some other Catholic Schools, in obedience to Gardiner's Catholic Relief Act of the previous year. His second wife was the widow of Hepenstal, the "Walking Gallows." Duigenan died at Sandymount in 1816, and bequeathed his fortune to his first wife's nephew, Baron Smith. It was a brave thing of Duigenan when he had become a prominent man to go and reside in Chancery-lane amongst the lawyers, within a stone's throw of the lane in which he was reared as a poor boy; and it was not less brave of him to be a liberal subscriber to St. Bride's parish school. He was not ashamed to look back at the rock whence he was hewn. Very few parvenus have this sort of nobility.

NOTE D. PAGE XLIV.

GRATTAN AND FITZGIBBON'S COLLEGE COURSE.

The life-long competition between Fitzgibbon and Grattan was so individual and so keen, and commenced so early, that the following quotations from the College books, now for the first time given, will probably be interesting. Can any other University produce a corresponding record?

The two splendid rivals, it will be remembered, carried far into public life their early friendship. Fitzgibbon was as earnest as Grattan for Irish parliamentary independence. He was one of Grattan's most fervid eulogists, and it was Grattan that got him made Attorney-General in 1785. Their first serious difference was on the Navigation Act in 1786; three years later they fell out finally on the Regency Bill.

EXTRACTS FROM THE MATRICULATION
BOOK, T.C.D.

"1763.

"John Fitzgibbon, F.C., June 6th (next class). Educated
by Mr. Ball. Tutor—Mr. Law. Class begins July 8th, 1763.

"Brought over to this class, with five others, John Fitzgibbon, F.C.

"1763.

"Henry Grattan, F.C., Nov. 1st, 6 a.m. Educated by
Dr. Campbell. Tutor—Mr. Law."

These entries show that Fitzgibbon and Grattan entered college the same year, under the same college tutor, and that they were in the same class. They graduated in the same Commencements. They were, moreover, in the same division, sitting within two of each other, Fitzgibbon, from his earlier entrance, sitting above Grattan in the hall. This proximity gives even a quicker interest to their neck and neck race, as detailed in the following record of their examination judgments:—

EXTRACTS FROM THE EXAMINATION BOOK, T.C.D.
"1764.
"Hilary Term—Junior Freshmen.
"1st Division—Mr. Stock, Examiner.
"Mr. Fitzgibbon, 3 V.B. 1 B. (i.e., Valde Bene and Bene).
"Mr. Grattan, V.B. in omnibus. Præmium.

"Easter Examinations, May, 1764.
"8th Division—Mr. Smyth, Examiner.
"Mr. Grattan, V.B. in omn. Certificate.
"Names of scholars who missed (i.e., did not go in for) the Examination.
"Mr. Fitzgibbon.

"Trinity Term.
"1st Division—Mr. Connor, Examiner.
"Mr. Fitzgibbon, 3 V.B., 1 B. Præmium.
"Mr. Grattan, V.B. in omnibus. Certificate.
"Remarkably diligent at Greek Lecture—
"Mr. Grattan.

"Michaelmas Examinations, October 19th, 1764.
"1st Division—Mr. Connor, Examiner.
"Mr. Fitzgibbon, V.B. in omnibus. Certificate.
"Mr. Grattan, 3 V.B., 1 B.

"1765.
"Hilary Term Examinations—Senior Freshmen.
"1st Division—Mr. Smyth, Examiner.
"Mr. Fitzgibbon, V.B. in omn. Præmium.
"Mr. Grattan, 3 V.B., 1 B.

"Hilary Term—Senior Freshmen.
"Mr. Fitzgibbon, Th. for G.L.
"Mr. Grattan, Th. for G.L.

"Easter Term Examinations, April, 1765.
"1st Division—Mr. Lucas, Examiner.
"Mr. Fitzgibbon, V.B. in omn. Certificate.
"Mr. Grattan, V.B. in omn. Præmium.

"Trinity Term Examinations, June 21st, 1765.
"1st Division—Mr. Stock, Examiner.
"Mr. Grattan, senior, 5 V.B. Certificate.
"Missed the Examination—Mr. Fitzgibbon.

"Easter and Trinity Terms—Senior Freshmen.
"Mr. Fitzgibbon, Th. for G.L.
"Mr. Grattan, senior, Th. for G.L.

[N.B.—"Th." means *thanks*, "Rem. Th." *remarkable thanks*, and "G.L." *Greek* and *Latin*.]

"Michaelmas Examinations, October 21st, 1765.
"Mr. Smyth, Examiner.
"Log. Math. Gr. Lat. Th.
"Mr. Fitzgibbon, V.B. in omnibus. Certificate.
"Mr. Grattan, senior, 4 V.B., 1 B. (in Th.)

"Michaelmas Term—Junior Sophisters.
"Mr. Fitzgibbon, Rem. Th. for G.L.
"1766.
"Christmas Examinations (generally called 'Hilary'), January 20th, 1766.
"Junior Sophisters—Mr. Law, Examiner.
"Log. Math. Astr. Phys. Eth. Gr. Lat. Th.
"Mr. Fitzgibbon, 5 V.B., optime in Ethics. Præmium.
"Mr. Grattan, senior, V.B. in omnibus.

"Easter Examinations, April 18th, 1766.
"Mr. Forsayeth, Examiner.
"Mr. Fitzgibbon, 5 V.B., 2 B.
"Mr. Grattan, senior, 2 V.B., 3 B. (2 blanks).

"Michaelmas Term Examinations (Degree Examination), October 20th, 1766.
"Mr. Forsayeth, Examiner.
"Candidates.
"Mr. Fitzgibbon, 5 V.B., 1 S.B., 2 B.
"Mr. Grattan, V.B. all through."

This table of judgments bears out Archbishop Magee's statement in his funeral sermon on Lord Clare, that Grattan was best in the first and Fitzgibbon in the closing years of their college course; while Grattan came to the front again at the Degree Examination. The table exhibits also the old system of awarding examination premiums in T.C.D.; and it shows the then curriculum in the Sophister year. It shows also that Fellow-Commoners obtained their B.A. degree on a shortened Academic course. Grattan entered in November, 1763, he answered for his degree in October, 1766, i.e., at the close of his Junior Sophister year—and he took his B.A. in Spring, 1767.

The Matriculation Book shows that Fitzgibbon was educated at Ball's famous school, under the old Round Tower, in Great Ship-street.[106] Grattan was educated in the same school along with Fitzgibbon, and was removed from it shortly before entrance, as his "Life" tells, and as the Matriculation Book also shows. Fitzgibbon was born in 1749, and, therefore, was only fourteen or fifteen years of age when he was collaring Grattan, who was three years his senior. Fitzgibbon was reared in his father's house,[107] in Stephen-street, and Grattan was reared within a few yards of

[106] For a full account of this school see "The Old Latin Schools of Dublin," by the Editor.

[107] Fitzgibbon's father had been a Catholic, and was intended for the priesthood. He

him, in his father's house in Chancery-lane. In the same school, at the same time, were educated Macaulay Boyd, one of the reputed authors of Junius' Letters (son of Alexander Macaulay, who lived in Great Ship-street); Sir Samuel Bradstreet, the steady patriot, who procured "Habeas Corpus" for Ireland, and who lived in the same street; and John Forbes, who lived in the same street with the Fitzgibbons, was a thorough supporter of Grattan, a forward champion of Catholic claims, and the resolute and successful assailant of the Pension List.

The University conferred its LL.D. *Honoris Causâ* on Fitzgibbon—notwithstanding his anti-Hutchinson performances. It had no honorary degree for Grattan, and the loss is to its own muster-roll of fame. The name would have honoured and ennobled the Register.

NOTE E.

LISTS OF THE SECRETARIES OF STATE, CHANCELLORS OF THE EXCHEQUER,SPEAKERS OF THE IRISH HOUSE OF COMMONS, AND CHIEF SECRETARIES.

PRINCIPAL SECRETARIES OF STATE—CALLED ALSO PRINCIPAL SECRETARIES OF THE COUNCIL, AND KEEPERS OF THE PRIVY SIGNET OR PRIVY SEAL—FROM THE RESTORATION.

1661, Sir Paul Davys; 1678, Sir John Davys; 1690, Sir R. Southwell; 1702, Sir E. Southwell and his son, 1775, Thomas Carter (Master of the Rolls); 1760, Philip Tisdall (Attorney-General); 1777, John Hely Hutchinson (Provost, &c.); 1795, Lord Glentworth; 1796, Hon. Thomas Pelham; 1797, Robert Stewart (Castlereagh); 1801, Charles Abbott (afterwards Speaker of English House of Commons, and Lord Colchester.)

*   *   *   *   *

IRISH CHANCELLORS OF THE EXCHEQUER.

1761, William Yorke—*vice* Anthony Malone; 1763, William Gerard Hamilton ("Single Speech"); 1784, John Foster (Speaker, &c.); 1785, Sir John Parnell; 1799, Isaac Corry; 1804, John Foster; 1806, Sir John Newport; 1807, John Foster; 1811, Wellesley Pole; 1812, William Fitzgerald; 1817, Nicholas Vansittart.

*   *   *   *   *

SPEAKERS OF THE IRISH HOUSE OF COMMONS SINCE THE RESTORATION.

1661, Sir Audley Mervin; 1692, Sir R. Levinge, H.M.'s Solicitor-General; 1695, Rt. Hon. Robert Rochfort, Attorney-General; 1703, Broderick Allen; 1710, Hon. John Forster; 1715, Rt. Hon. Wm. Connolly; 1729, Sir Ralph Gore; 1733, Hon. Henry Boyle (Lord Shannon); 1756, Rt. Hon. John Ponsonby; 1771, Rt. Hon. Edmund Sexton Pery (Lord Pery); 1785, Rt. Hon. John Foster.

---

and his wife Eleanor are buried in St. Bride's churchyard, without any sort of monument or tombstone.

CHIEF SECRETARIES TO LORD LIEUTENANTS.

Year.	Chief Secretary.	Lord Lieutenant.
1703.	Sir E. Southwell (also Principal Secretary of State).	Duke of Ormonde.
1707.	Joshua Dawson.	Lord Pembroke.
1709.	George Bubb Doddington (also Clerk of the Pells).	Lord Wharton.
1711.	— — Southwell.	Duke of Ormonde again.
1713.	Sir John Stanley.	Duke of Shrewsbury.
1724.	Thomas Clutterbuck.	Lord Carteret.
1731.	Walter Carey.	Duke of Dorset.
1738.	Edward Walpole, and Nicholas Bonfoy. (This was the Mr. Walpole who had the escapade with the notorious Letitia Pilkington).	Duke of Devonshire.
1740.	Henry Legg, and Nicholas Bonfoy.	Duke of Devonshire.
1742.	Lord Duncannon and Nicholas Bonfoy, Esq.	Duke of Devonshire.
1745.	B. Liddell (a Cornish M.P.), and William Bristow.	Lord Chesterfield.
1747.	— — Wayte.	Lord Harrington.
1751.	Lord G. Sackville (also Clerk of the Council, and Keeper of Phœnix Park).	Duke of Dorset again.
1755.	Robert Maxwell.	Marquis of Hartington.
1757.	Richard Rigby (also Master of the Rolls).	Duke of Bedford.
1761.	"Single Speech" Hamilton (also Chancellor of the Exchequer).	Lord Halifax.
1763.	Hamilton again, and Lord Drogheda.	Lord Northumberland.
1765.	Edward Thurlow.	Lord Weymouth, who did not come.
1765.	Lord Beauchamp.	Lord Hertford.
1766.	Lord Aug. Hervey.	Lord Bristol (did not come).
1767.	Sir G., afterwards Lord McCartney (Governor of Madras), and Lord Fk. Campbell.	Marquis Townshend.
1772.	Sir John Blacquiere (also Alnager, and afterwards Lord Blacquiere).	Lord Hartcourt.
1777.	Sir Rd. Heron (his Excellency's land agent; also Searcher, Packer, and Gauger of the Port of Cork).	Lord Buckinghamshire.
1780.	W. Eden (afterwards Lord Auckland).	Lord Carlisle.

1782.	Colonel Fitzpatrick.	Duke of Portland.
1782.	Lord Grenville (also Chief Remembrancer, with £4,000 a year).	Lord Temple, Buckingham.
1783.	Thomas Pelham and William Wyndham.	Lord Northington.
1784.	Thomas Orde (afterwards Lord Bolton).	Duke of Rutland.
1787.	Alleyne Fitzherbert (afterwards Lord St. Helens).	Marquis of Buckingham again.
1790.	Major Hobart (afterwards Lord Buckinghamshire).	Lord Westmoreland.
1795.	Syl. Douglas (Lord Glenbervie).	Lord Fitzwilliam.
1795.	G. Damer (afterwards Lord Milton). T. Pelham (afterwards Lord Chichester).	Lord Camden.
1798.	Lord Castlereagh.	Lord Cornwallis.
1801.	Charles Abbott (afterwards Speaker of English House of Commons, and Lord Colchester); W. Wickham; Sir Evan Napean (Treasurer of Irish Exchequer); Nicholas Vansittart (afterwards Lord Bexley); Charles Long (afterwards Lord Farnborough).	Lord Hardwick.
1801.	W. Elliott.	Duke of Bedford.
1807.	Sir A. Wellesley, Robert Dundas (afterwards Lord Melville), Wellesley Pole (also Chancellor of the Irish Exchequer, and afterwards Lord Maryborough).	Duke of Richmond.
1812.	Sir R. Peel.	Lord Whitworth.
1818.	Charles Grant (Lord Glenleg).	Lord Talbot.
1821.	Henry Goulburn.	Marquis Wellesley.
1827.	W. Lamb (Lord Melbourne).	Marquis Wellesley.
1828.	Lord F. Levenson Gower (Lord Ellesmere).	Marquis of Anglesey and Duke of Northumberland.
1830.	Sir H. Hardinge (afterwards Lord Hardinge).	Marquis of Anglesey again.
1830.	Edward Stanley (Lord Derby).	Marquis of Anglesey again.
1833.	Cam Hobhouse, E. J. Littleton (Lord Hatherton.)	Marquis of Wellesley again.
1834.	Sir H. Hardinge again.	Lord Haddington, and Lord Mulgrave, and Lord Fortescue.
1834.	G. F. W. Howard (Lord Carlisle).	

1841.	Lord Elliott (Earl St. Germains).	Lord De Grey.
1845.	Sir Thos. Freemantle.	Lord Heytesbury.
1846.	Lord Lincoln.	Lord Bessborough.
1846.	Henry Labouchere.	Lord Bessborough.
1847.	Sir William Somerville.	Lord Clarendon.
1853.	Lord Naas.	Lord Eglinton.
1854.	Sir John Young.	Lord St. Germains.
1855.	Edward Horsman, and Hon. H. Herbert.	Lord Carlisle.
1858.	Lord Naas.	Lord Eglinton again.
1860.	Edward Cardwell.	Lord Carlisle again.
1862.	Sir R. Peel.	Lord Carlisle.
1865.	Do. Do.	Lord Kimberley.
1866.	Chichester Fortescue (afterwards Lord Carlingford).	Lord Kimberley.
1867.	Lord Naas (afterwards Lord Mayo).	Duke of Abercorn.
1868.	Chichester Fortescue again.	Lord Spencer.
1871.	Marquis of Hartington.	Lord Spencer.
1873.	Sir M. H. Beach.	Duke of Abercorn again.
1879.	James Lowther.	Duke of Marlborough.
1880.	W. E. Forster.	Lord Cowper.

N.B.—It is instructive to note how very few of the here-mentioned eighty Chief Secretaries, the persons mainly entrusted with the government of the country for 180 years, belonged to the country, or had any real knowledge of its condition and requirements. If the other kingdoms of the earth were administered on this principle, the "*quam parvâ sapientiâ*" would excite no astonishment.

INTRODUCTION.

Although this work was published anonymously, there never was any question as to who was its author. It was always known to be the production of Provost Hely Hutchinson, and its first appearance was greeted with two different sorts of reception. It was burned by the Common Hangman so effectually, that Mr. Flood said he would give a thousand pounds for a copy and that the libraries of all the three branches of the legislature could not produce a copy[108]—and at the same time it "earned Mr. Hely Hutchinson's pardon from Irish patriotism for his subserviency to the Court and Lord Townshend."[109] The book was the outcome of the stubborn inability of English rulers to interpret the face of this country; and the first sketch of the publication was the papers which the author contributed to Lord Lieutenant Buckinghamshire in 1779 as to the cause of the existing ruin here and as to its cure. The purport of the Letters was to exhibit, calmly and seriously, and as by a friend to both countries, the grievous oppressions which the greedy spirit of English trade inflicted on the commerce, industries, and manufactures of Ireland during the century and a quarter that extended from the Restoration of Charles II. to the rise of Grattan. The author draws all his statements from the Statute Books and Commons Journals of both kingdoms, while he does not fail to support his own conclusions and comments by State Papers and Statistical Returns that possess an authority equal to that of the Statutes. He lays the whole length and breadth of the position steadily and searchingly before the Viceroy's eyes. He shows him that the then state of Ireland teemed with every circumstance of national poverty, while the country itself abounded in the conditions of national prosperity. Of productiveness there was no lack; but land produce was greatly reduced in value; wool had fallen one half, wheat one third, black cattle in the same proportion, and hides in a much greater. There were no buyers, tenants were not to be found, landlords lost one fourth of their rents, merchants could do no business, and within two years over twenty thousand manufacturers in this city were disemployed, beggared, and supported by alms. All this was after a period of fourscore years of profound internal peace—and the question was, what was the cause of it?

This is what the author sets himself to investigate in the Letters, and in regard of sweep of survey, historic retrospect, statistical quotation, and close economic

---

[108] Mr. Blackburne's "Causes of the Decadence of the Industries of Ireland," p. 19.

There are two copies of the work in the College Library, both of which have been recently obtained, and from one of them, by the obliging indulgence of the Provost and Board, the present re-issue is taken.

[109] Froude—"English in Ireland," vol. ii., p. 228.

comment, the investigation leaves little to be desired. The Provost is anxious, in the first place, to point out that it was not absentee rents, salaries, profits of offices, and pensions that caused the decline—and this forestalling admonition is no more than what might be expected from a man who was such an insatiable trafficker in places, and salaries, and profits, and pensions. He admits that these things made the decline more rapid, but a "more radical" cause was to be assigned for a malady that arose out of the constitution itself. He maintains that Ireland was flourishing, prosperous, and wealthy under James and Charles I., and that after the Restoration it was one of the most improved and improving spots in Europe. This is a somewhat poetical view, especially when we remember how Strafford ruined the landowners and destroyed the wool trade; but wretched as was the condition of the people under the Stuarts, it may have been less unendurable than the condition under "a succession of five excellent sovereigns." In truth, talking about the perpetually developed prosperity of the Irish people under the several successions of English misrule is the very irony of pharisaism, although the recital is a stereotyped phrase of English officials from the Tudor *employés* down to those of our own days,[110] none of whom ever fail to find "the strings of the Irish harp all in tune."

[110] See the State Papers of Henry VIII., and the official certificates almost ever since. See also Lord O'Hagan's Address to the Social Science Congress in Dublin, 1881. If any of these pronouncements were right, it would be difficult to discover any room for future improvement. All of these glowing congratulations were, however, invariably exposed and exploded by sober contemporary historians and observers, and the O'Hagan passage illustrates the process. His lordship said: "I have indicated to you the results of honest effort by Irishmen of this generation in obtaining for their country amended laws, cheap and facile justice—education liberal, unconditioned, and available to all—... increased provision for the national health and comfort—and security in his possessions and encouragement to his industry for the tiller of the soil. In the midst of many troubles and much discouragement, these have been steps of real cheering progress—improvements, permanently conquered from the past, and auspicious, as they will be fruitful, of a happier future." Compare with this charming view the following versions.

In his speech in the adjourned debate on the Address in the House of Commons, January, 1881, Mr. Shaw, M.P. for Cork County, showed the value of this "real cheering progress," and of the "permanent improvements and increased provisions for the national health and comfort." "Within three or four months," said Mr. Shaw, "I have gone through various parts of the country, and I must say this—I did not think it possible for human beings to exist as I found tenant-farmers existing in the West of Ireland.... It is a disgrace to the landlords, it is a disgrace to the Government, it is a disgrace to every institution in the country to think of it that now for years, for generations, this cry year after year has been coming up from the people."

In the debate on the 28th of January MR. GLADSTONE said that "there are still hundreds of thousands in Ireland who live more or less on the brink of starvation, and that forty years ago that was the case not with hundreds of thousands but with millions."

A writer in the current number of the *Quarterly Review*, after picturing the maddened and disturbed state of the country, adds:—

"And all this with between four and five hundred suspects in gaols with an army of 50,000 men in the country, with Land Bills, Coercion Bills, Proclamations, new magisterial boards, the island parcelled out into military districts, spies, informers, and all the endless appliances of a Liberal Government in full operation."

In some periods the distress may have been more intense than in others, and in all periods there were not wanting instances of individual aggrandisement—but the general wretchedness remained fast fixed. England has been a constant source of woe to Ireland, and suffering is the badge of all our tribe. In any strict assize Hutchinson would be laughed out of Court for essaying to plead the wealth and prosperity of Ireland directly after the devastations of the Carews and Mountjoys, after the Desmond and Ulster confiscations and evictions, and after the Cromwellian atrocities. Hutchinson knew quite well what the condition of the people was all through; but it suited him, rhetorically, to cut out a corner of the picture and to colour that corner very highly. Graziers used to make a good thing of their cattle and of their wool, and economic returns of their exports showed pleasant balance sheets; but graziers were not the Irish people any more than Manchester is England now. In fact, they were chiefly English landowners here, and the extent of their exports is only the measure of the misery which they left unpitied and unrelieved. This, however, was not the philosophy which Hutchinson wanted to preach; and he was far too clear-headed a man to make a mistake as to what he wanted to say. He accordingly lays hold on the figures that set off his argument, and out of fancy premises he draws a solid conclusion which in no sense needed such controvertible data. What was certain was that Ireland possessed the conditions of prosperity, and that it teemed with actual poverty. The question was, what caused this contradiction? The answer was, England caused it; and this is the answer which Hutchinson plainly and nakedly gives. In all the rest of his book—i.e. from Letter III. to the close—he sustains this thesis with a directness that cannot be gainsayed or resisted. Having related the efforts of Strafford—one of the most malignant enemies that Ireland ever encountered—to crush the wool trade here in the time of Charles I., Hutchinson comes to the acts of the English under Charles II. and William III.

Charles, so far as he could have a liking for anything outside his pleasures, had a liking for Ireland; and William feeling that he had already done Ireland wrong enough, was disposed at last to be merciful and liberal towards her; but both of the kings were overborne by their English parliaments.

In 1663, the English Act "for encouragement of Trade"! contained an insidious clause, imposing a penalty of £2 on each head of Irish cattle, and 10s. on each sheep imported into England between July and December. In 1666, the "Act against importing cattle from Ireland and other places beyond seas, and fish taken by foreigners" was passed, and to annoy the king the importation was termed a "nuisance."[111] This Act was made perpetual by the "Act of 1678, prohibiting the

---

See, too, what Mr. Justice O'Hagan said in his judgment on the Stacpoole leases. It is not very easy to reconcile these four unassailable statements of facts with the smooth optimism of the ex-Lord Chancellor, although without question the "Conquests" enumerated by him have been, as he says, won. The truth is that these specialist statistics are no more a real index of the condition of the country than a brick is an index of the quality of a house. There is no use in attempting to deny that England—both when meaning well and meaning ill—has kept Ireland in a deplorable condition.

[111] Concerning this debate "Pepys' Diary," vol. iv., p. 109, records—1666—October 8th:—"The House did this day order to be engrossed the Bill against importing Irish Cat-

importation of cattle from Ireland." This latter Act was not repealed until the 5th of George III., when the permission was granted for seven years; the permission was made perpetual by the 16th of the same reign.

Carte[112] relates at length and with an honest sympathy with Ireland, the whole incident of 1663-8. He tells how the Duke of Ormond, who was then Lord Lieutenant here, together with his valiant son, Lord Ossory, strove manfully for this country, and how he prevailed with the king to delay the obnoxious measure. He mentions also Ormond's noble enterprise in establishing at Clonmel the flourishing Walloon woollen manufactory. Carte records likewise how, in 1666, the Dublin people, when scant of money by virtue of English jealousy, sent over a contribution of 30,000 fat oxen to feed the Londoners who had suffered by the great fire, and how ungraciously the generous boon was received by the ill-mannered English victuallers and by their bribed spokesmen in high places.[113]

Notwithstanding this benevolence of the Irish people, the English persisted in ruining their cattle trade, and before the end of William's reign they passed a further law to ruin the Irish woollen trade. This was in 1699, and the long depression and degradation which resulted from it prove, says Hutchinson, "this melancholy truth, that a country will sooner recover from the miseries and devastations occasioned by war, invasion, rebellion, and massacre, than from laws restraining the commerce, discouraging the manufactures, fettering the industry, and, above all, breaking the spirit of the people."

---

tle—a thing, it seems, carried on by the Western Parliament men wholly against the sense of most of the rest of the House; who think if you do this you give the Irish again cause to rebel. Thus plenty on both sides makes us mad."

P. 135—1666. October 27th:—"Thence to talk about publique business; he [Lord Belassis] tells me how the two Houses begun to lie troublesome, the Lords to have quarrels one with another. My Lord Duke of Buckingham having said to the Lord Chancellor (who is against the passing of the Bill for prohibiting the bringing over of Irish cattle) that whoever was against the Bill was there led to it by an Irish interest or an Irish understanding, which is as much as to say he is a foole. This bred heat from my Lord Chancellor, and something he [Buckingham] said did offend my Lord of Ossory (my Lord Duke of Ormonde's son), and they two had hard words, upon which the latter sends a challenge to the former; of which the former complains to the House, and so the business is to be heard on Monday." Clarendon and Carte attribute cowardice to Buckingham in the matter. Both he and Ossory were sent to the Tower. The Bill, as noticed above, was subsequently passed.

[112] "Life of Ormond," vol. iv., p. 234, &c.

[113] Ten years later Dublin sent out a cargo of provisions valued at £937 13s. to New England, and the benevolence was gratefully and gracefully commemorated in 1880 by Captain Potter, of the *Constellation*, when he brought over America's consignment to our famishing agriculturists, and received the honorary freedom of our city. It may be noted, too, that ten years before the contribution to London, Dublin sent a relief amounting to £1,000 to the Waldenses, when suffering from the persecution of the Duke of Savoy. The last-named collection was made by a Cromwellian Fellow of Trinity College, the Rev. Samuel Mather, an excellent man, who on the Restoration was thrown into a Dublin prison, probably the "Black Dog," for declining to sign the Act of Uniformity. The New England collection was made by his brother, the Rev. Nathaniel Mather, Minister of the New-row Meeting-house. The collection for London was made by the Duke of Ormond.

This melancholy truth the Provost goes on to illustrate and enforce, and he does this by reciting the facts from the beginning, and from year to year continually, as they are recorded in the journals of Parliament. The restriction of the cattle trade in 1666, when the people, in reliance on the continuance of the trade, had greatly increased their live-stocks, compelled the Irish to develop their wool trade. They had been encouraged by their English rulers to devote their energies to this industry, because the "country was so fertile by nature, and so advantageously situated for trade and navigation." Suddenly a Bill was introduced into the English parliament in 1697 and passed in 1699, restraining the exportation of woollen manufactures from Ireland, and beseeching His Majesty "in the most public and effectual way that may be, to declare to all his subjects of Ireland, that the growth and increase of the woollen manufacture hath long, and will ever be, looked upon with jealousy by all his subjects of this [England] kingdom," and further "to enjoin all those he employed in Ireland to make it their care and use their utmost diligence, to hinder the exportation of wool from Ireland except to be imported hither [to England], and for the discouraging the woollen manufacture," &c. To this address King William gave the ever memorable reply: "*I shall do all that in me lies to discourage the woollen trade in Ireland, and to encourage the linen manufacture there;*[114] *and to promote the trade of England;*" and he wrote to the Lords Justices over here to have a measure to that effect passed in the Irish parliament. The Lords Justices accordingly made "a quickening speech" to both Houses; a Bill for their acceptance was transmitted from the Castle, and the Irish parliament, in which the Williamite influence was dominant, passed the measure that annihilated the industry and prosperity of their country.[115] By this law an additional duty of twenty per cent. was imposed on broadcloth, and of ten per cent. on all new draperies except friezes; and the law which was enacted in January, 1699, was to be in force for three years. This law, prohibitive as it was, did not, however, satisfy England. In the June of the same year the English parliament passed a perpetual law, not overtaxing but expressly prohibiting the exportation from Ireland of all goods made of or mixed with wool, except to England and Wales, and with the licence of the Revenue Commissioners. Previous English Acts had made the duties on the importation into England practically prohibitive, and therefore the last Act operated as a suppression of exportation. The Irish were already prevented from importing dye-stuffs from the colonies, and from exporting their woollen manufactures thither. What England wanted was, not a fair competition with Ireland, but a monopoly; she was resolved to prevent Ireland not merely from underselling her in foreign markets, but from selling there at all.

The natural and actual result of this exorbitant greed was that the Irish people were driven to have recourse to the method of "running the wool," i.e. smuggling it away to foreign markets. The severest penalties were enacted by the British legislature and by the Irish House of Commons against this practice, but they were enacted in vain. It was impossible to seal up a country of whose thirty-two counties

---

[114] This encouragement of the linen trade here proved a hypocrisy and imposture. The linen trade was never an equivalent for the wool trade.

[115] Excepting, perhaps, Poyning's Act, and the Act of Union, this was the most disgraceful Act ever passed by an Irish Parliament.

nineteen are maritime and the rest washed by fine rivers that empty themselves into the sea. The wool running prevailed to an immense extent, and by means of it France, Germany, and Spain were able to undersell England in the foreign markets, and England lost millions of pounds by virtue of the Irish contraband supplies. The market price of Europe mocked the English importation duties, and more than defeated the prohibition. At last, in 1739, after forty years of oppression here and loss to herself, England relaxed the severity of the restrictions, and as her own House of Commons Journal acknowledges, this relaxation was made for the benefit of the English woollen manufactures. For the twenty-three years that succeeded King William's pledge to ruin the best trade in this country, there is an unvaried record of the depression and misery of the Irish people, and during all this period and in the face of all this acknowledgment, there was not even a proposal of any law, saving one about casks for butter and tallow, to encourage our manufactures, or to tolerate our trade, or to let the country revive. There was a native parliament here, and why did they exhibit this wondrous apathy? "Because," says our author, "it was well understood by both Houses of Parliament that they had no power to remove those restraints which prohibited trade and discouraged manufactures, and that any application for that purpose would at that time have only offended the people on one side of the Channel without bringing any relief to those on the other."

In 1723, the petition of the woollen weavers and clothiers of Dublin forced from the Lord Lieutenant in his speech from the throne a recommendation to find out some employment for the poor, but neither petition nor speech produced any effect. From 1723 to 1729 the distress continued; in the latter year it was aggravated by a famine. The scarcity was caused not by any blight of the land produce, but by the despair of the farmers; for when exportation is prohibited, and the manufacturing class at home is without employment and without money to buy, farmers will abandon tillage and dearth must ensue. In a few years more there was another scarcity of food, and then the Lord Lieutenant congratulated the country on the success of the linen trade, and recommended the encouragement of tillage. Nothing, however, was done to alter the conditions on which the improvement of the tillage depended, "because the Commons said that the evil was out of their reach and that the poor were not employed because they were discouraged by restrictive laws from working up the materials of the country." Thus matters went on from bad to worse until after the peace of 1745, when there came an influx of money, by which the debt that had been contracted for England's Jacobite war of 1715 was paid off in 1754, and the result of this discharge was increased burdens on the country without any accompanying relief to commerce and industries. The Treasury balance led, in 1753, to a dispute as to the right of disposing of it between the King and the Commons; and this dispute was the first beginning of parliamentary life in Ireland.[116] To get rid of the redundancy and to leave the less for English pensions and Government salaries, works of local improvement were undertaken, and these undertakings, so far as they were carried out, helped to give employment and to stimulate agriculture.

---

[116] See page xlii, note, and 16.

This, however, was but a partial and insufficient remedy for the universal distress, and small as it was, it was obtained against the will of the English Government. No real relief was conferred on the country, and within a couple of years more the revenue fell off, and £20,000 was voted for the relief of the poor.

In 1757[117] it was thought an amazing feat when Pery carried his Land Carriage and Coal Acts; and then, in 1761, came the augmentation of the army.[118] On the breaking out of the Spanish war, there was a fresh vote of credit, and still no relief to manufacturers or to agriculturists. This distress, caused by English-made laws, Hutchinson points out, produced the White Boys, and for the cure of this distress an increased attention to the Charter Schools was recommended. By 1771 the National Debt had largely increased, while income had diminished, and in a couple of years more the linen trade was rapidly declining, while pensions and charges on the establishment were greatly increased.

The Provost dwells on the illustrative fact, that, whether the Debt was increased or diminished, and however much the pensions and salaries were multiplied, the distress and wretchedness of the body of the people continued the same. The linen manufacture for a while prospered, and afforded a limited relief in a few places; but tillage was declining, and destitution was all round. The distress was noticed in the House, but nothing effectual was attempted, and Hutchinson cannot refrain from exclaiming: "Can the history of any other fruitful country on the globe, enjoying peace for fourscore years, and not visited by plague or pestilence, produce so many recorded instances of the poverty and wretchedness, and of the reiterated want and misery of the lower orders of the people? There is no such example in ancient or modern story. If the ineffectual endeavours by the representatives of those poor people to give them employment and food, had not left sufficient memorials of their wretchedness; if their habitations, apparel, and food, were not sufficient proofs, I should appeal to the human countenance for my voucher, and rest the evidence on that hopeless despondency that hangs on the brow of unemployed industry."

All these restrictions were enacted by England, not from any actual loss that she had sustained by Irish competition, but from an apprehension of loss. Hutchinson shows how groundless the apprehension was, and he protests against the iniquity of sacrificing the happiness of a great and ancient kingdom, and the welfare of millions of its people, to guard against an imagined decrease in the value of English land. If wool-spinning was cheaper in Ireland than in England, that was because the Irish operatives had to live on food—"potatoes and milk, or more frequently water"[119]—with which the English would not be content; but wages

[117] See page xlii, note, and 19.

[118] It was on the Army Augmentation Bill that Hutchinson made one of his early "strides in apostasy." It was on this occasion also that Ireland was for the first time called upon to contribute to England's war expenses. She passed a vote of credit for £200,000. See pages 20, 21.

[119] The condition of the people would thus seem to have declined from what it was a century before. In 1672, Petty stated in his "Political Anatomy," that the drink of the Irish people was milk, and in winter small beer or water; and that their food was bread made into cakes, with eggs and rancid butter, and with muscles, cockles, and oysters, on the sea-

and the cost of producing would increase with the opening of trade, and with the increase of manufactures. England's greedy monopoly was sinking the Irish people, while fair trade would really lessen the cheap labour competition which the English masters professed to dread. An open wool trade in Ireland would, moreover, be mainly carried on by English capitalists and by English shipping, just as in ancient Egypt, China, and Hindostan, the export trade used to be conducted by foreigners; and just as in the victualling trade of Ireland, the natives were but factors to the English. On every side, therefore, the English themselves suffered as much by the restrictions as the Irish, and they would be, if they could but see it, proportionate gainers by the removal of the restrictions. Hutchinson goes on to show that England gets one-third of the wealth of Ireland, and that she would get more than the half of the benefit of the wool trade; but that even so the country would be the better for the small share of the gains that would be allowed to remain with her. Agriculture would be encouraged, and manufactures would be promoted; and there would be a circulation of money amongst the people. Taxes were proportionately heavier in Ireland than in England, when the annual earnings, expenditure, rentals, circulating specie, and personal property of the two countries were compared. The English were mistaken in some of the calculations on which they grounded the commercial restrictions, and they would be commercial gainers by the removal of the restrictions; but it was not for the benefit of England, and it was for the benefit of Ireland, that the Provost demanded free and open commerce for the produce and manufactures of this country. This was what he claimed and argued for, and this was what he very largely helped to obtain for Ireland; and this was the service that won him back a great deal of the popularity which he had forfeited by his hired subserviency to the English party.

There is a good deal of repetition in the Provost's book as we have it, but this is accounted for by the fact that the book was originally published in the form of letters.[120] The repetitions, moreover, are not altogether artistic blemishes, for they are made to intensify, and, as it were, to multiply, the identical facts by presenting them in fresh connections. This is notably the case in regard of the Provost's doublings back on the wool trade, and on the linen trade, and on England's deal-shore parts.

[120] There are also several inaccuracies in the printed edition, which are reproduced as they stand. *E.g.*, in page 35 "between £12,000 and £13,000" is set down as an increase on £1,100,000; and Petty's "Survey" is throughout put for his Political Anatomy. In the note to page 53 the literal misprints in the Greek quotation are corrected. The line is given "as Homer quoted by Longinus," and as if it were a Homeric line, but it is not a hexameter at all. The quotation joins the beginning of one line to a portion of another, and it is needless to say that the break was duly notified by Longinus, though apparently it was not perceived by the Provost.

The passage occurs in the 17th book of the Odyssey, V.V. 323-3:—

    "Ἥμισυ γαρ τ᾽ ἀρετῆς ἀποαίνυται εὐρυόπα Ζευς
    Ἀνέρος, ἐῦτ᾽ αν μιν κατα δουλιον ἦμαρ ἔλησιν."

Rendered by Pope,

    "Jove fix'd it certain, that whatever day
    Makes man a slave, takes half his worth away."

ings with Ireland in regard of both these trades. After the destruction of the cattle trade these were the two sources of industry left to this country, and therefore the record of the treatment and evolution of these trades is in fact the history of the commercial relations between England and this country. The Provost accordingly takes the wool and the linen trade as the fixed pillars of his discourse, and he interpolates the spaces between them with coincident statistics that illustrate his thesis. It is thus that in page 35 he comes back to the wool trade to show the falsehood of the English trade returns, which asserted that the trade "was set up here since the reduction of Ireland" by Cromwell. The trade had been a flourishing one in this country from the time of Edward III. Then in the Sixth Letter the Provost takes up the linen trade again, for the purpose of showing more emphatically, in the first place, that it was forced on Ireland as an equivalent for the loss of the wool trade; in the second place, that it was not at all an equivalent—and in the third place, that England before long broke her stipulations with this country, and so *discouraged* the hemp and linen manufacture of Ireland, that the Irish had to abandon the flax culture altogether. In 1705, leave was given to Ireland to export some sorts of linen to the colonies, but leave was not given to bring back dye stuffs or other colonial produce. In 1743, bounties were offered on exports of Irish linen, provided they were shipped from English ports; but there was already a duty of thirty per cent. on *foreign* linen imported into England; and thus Ireland was, of course, deprived of the colonial and other markets. Not till 1777 were the American markets opened to Ireland, and by that time the emigration of the Ulster linen-workers had become so enormous, that America was, in fact, a rival in the trade. What words can more offensively and more bitterly express the oppression of the country than this leave to trade with other countries? It took Grattan and Hussey Burgh "with their coats off," and it took the Volunteers with their motto "Free Trade, or — —," to sweep away this badge of slavery. All the time England was multiplying pensions and salaries here; she was levying taxes and draining rents; and, as Hutchinson clearly puts it, Ireland "was paying to Great Britain double the sum that she collects from the whole world in all the trade which Great Britain allows her. It would be difficult to find a similar instance in the history of mankind." Again and again the Provost comes back to point out the open tyranny and the underhand unfairness of England's commercial legislation for this country, and in the Seventh Letter he repeats that this legislation was a departure from the policy which was guaranteed by Magna Charta, and which had prevailed from the time of Edward III. When a supposed compensation was afterwards offered, it was no more than what Ireland had had before, and the liberty granted by Queen Anne was merely allowing us to do in regard of one manufacture what had previously been a right in every instance.

"At this earlier period, then," says Hutchinson, "the English commercial system and the Irish, so far as it depended upon the English statute law, was the same; and before this period, so far as it depended upon the common law and Magna Charta, it was also the same."

"This was the voice of nature," he adds, "and the dictate of sound and generous policy; it proclaimed to the nations that they should not give to strangers the bread of their own children; that the produce of the soil should support the inhabitants of the country; that their industry should be exercised on their own materials, and that the poor should be employed, clothed, and fed.

"This policy was liberal, just, and equal; it opened the resources and cultivated the strength of every part of the empire."

From this liberal and profitable policy, however, England departed towards the close of the seventeenth century, and manifold were the wrongs which the departure inflicted on this country. The Provost details these wrongs with the indignation of a patriot; he rails at the oppression which, by depriving the people of liberty, robbed them of half their vigour; but still as a courtier and as a Government man, he was able to *revere that conquest which has given to Ireland the Common Law and the Magna Charta of England.*" Why he revered the Conquest, when the Common Law and Magna Charta failed to protect the welfare of Ireland, the Provost does not state. Two things stand out clearly throughout the treatise—one is that Ireland, both as a producer and as a consumer, has been immensely profitable to England; and the other is that England has been the source of vast evil and suffering to Ireland. The purport of "The Commercial Restraints" is to set forth these two great truths, and the record may be read now without prejudice on one side of the Channel, and without panic or passion on the other. The teaching of the book ought to be palpable enough for the men of the present day. It ought to convince Englishmen that it is time for them to distrust their "resources of civilisation," and to let this country prosper; and it ought to remind Irishmen that they are the best judges of what they want, and that their road to prosperity is independence of English conceit, together with a sturdy development of their own native resources.

In and since Provost Hutchinson's time Ireland has won vast conquests from her oppressor, and she has won them all by the same weapon—firm and constitutional discontent. She has much to win still, and she will surely win it by the same method, while outside that method she is powerless. Free Trade and Parliamentary Independence were won without shedding a drop of blood, and the conditions of the fight for what is required now are far more propitious and hopeful than they were a century ago. Then, Ireland had to contend with an obstinate king, a wrong-headed minister, and a greedy nation; now, all these things are changed. The men of '82, no doubt, had at their back the Irish Volunteers that England feared, and there are no Irish Volunteers now; their place, however, is supplied by a more coercive force, and that force is the spirit of justice which is spreading through the Liberals of England, and is fed by the Liberals of Ireland. But even supposing that all these demands touching land, education, and autonomy, were granted, there still remains another object for Irishmen to work out, namely, the recreation of their home industries and manufactures. The land, after all, is not everything—all the people cannot live by it and out of it—and, as Hutchinson observes, no one industry is sufficient to maintain a numerous population in prosperity and comfort.

In past times, as a couple of months ago the Lord Lieutenant at Belfast, and Mr. Fawcett at Shoreditch, were saying,[121] all these industries in the country were

[121] See *Freeman's Journal*, Nov. 3 and Nov. 24, 1881.

prohibited by unjust and iniquitous legislation, and by a mass of vexatious restrictions; but there are no prohibitions now, and the country abounds with the conditions and materials of prosperity. Bishop Berkeley wrote, when the prohibiting laws had been seventy years in operation, and when the force that swept them away had not yet begun to breathe in the country. He regarded the laws with despair, and piteously bemoaned the destitution and degradation in which the people were fixed. His earnest exhortation to them was to compensate themselves for the loss of the foreign trade by developing home industries and manufactures; and he asked[122] whether the natives might not be able to effect their own prosperity and elevation, even though "there was a wall of brass a thousand cubits high round this kingdom?"

Lord Clare, in his Union speech, declared that Ireland made more progress in her eighteen years of freedom than ever nation made in the same period; and it will be now for the working-men of this generation to show that, in enterprise and trades-craft they are not degenerate from their half-taught forefathers who won Fitzgibbon's testimony. There is every ground for confident anticipation, that this year's National Exhibition will profoundly and widely strengthen the effort for the revival of our Native Industries, and it is with the desire to contribute somewhat to the all-important and patriotic impulse that "The Commercial Restraints of Ireland" is now reproduced by the publishers.

---

[122] *Querist*, 134.

THE COMMERCIAL RESTRAINTS
OF IRELAND CONSIDERED.

FIRST LETTER.

Dublin, 20th Aug., 1779.

My Lord,

You desire my thoughts on the affairs of Ireland, a subject little considered, and consequently not understood in England. The Lords and Commons of Great Britain have addressed his Majesty to take the distressed and impoverished state of this country into consideration; have called for information and resolved to pursue effectual methods for promoting the common strength, wealth, and commerce of both kingdoms, and his Majesty has been pleased to express in his speech from the throne his entire approbation of their attention to the present state of Ireland.

The occasion calls for the assistance of every friend of the British Empire, and those who can give material information are bound to communicate it. The attempt, however, is full of difficulty; it will require more than ordinary caution to write with such moderation as not to offend the prejudices of one country and with such freedom as not to wound the feelings of the other.

The present state of Ireland teems with every circumstance of national poverty. Whatever the land produces is greatly reduced in its value: wool is fallen one-half in its usual price, wheat one-third, black cattle of all kinds in the same proportion, and hides in a much greater. Buyers are not had without difficulty at those low rates, and from the principal fairs men commonly return with the commodities they brought there; rents are everywhere reduced—in many places it is impossible to collect them;—the farmers are all distressed, and many of them have failed; when leases expire tenants are not easily found; the landlord is often obliged to take his lands into his own hands for want of bidders at reasonable rents, and finds his estate fallen one-fourth in its value. The merchant justly complains that all business is at a stand, that he cannot discount his bills, and that neither money nor paper circulates. In this and the last year above twenty thousand manufacturers in this metropolis were reduced to beggary for want of employment, they were for a considerable length of time supported by alms, a part of the contribution came from England and this assistance was much wanting from the general distress of all ranks of people in this country. Public and private credit are annihilated, Parliament, that always raises money in Ireland on easy terms, when there is any to be borrowed in the country, in 1778, gave £7½ per cent. in annuities, which, in 1773 and 1775, were earnestly sought after at £6, then thought to be a very high rate. The expenses of a country nearly bankrupt must be inconsiderable; almost every branch of the revenue has fallen, and the receipts in the Treasury for the two years ending Lady-day, 1779, were less than those for the two years ending Lady-day, 1777, deducting the sums received on account of loans in each period, in a sum of £334,900 18s. 9½d. There was due on the 25th of March last, on the establishments, and for extraordinary expenses, an arrear amounting to £373,706 13s. 6½d.; a sum of £600,000 will probably be now wanting to supply the deficiencies on the establishments and extraordinary charges of government, and an annual sum of between £50,000 and £60,000 yearly to pay interest and annuities. In the last session £466,000 was borrowed. If the sum wanting could now be raised, the debt would be increased in a sum of above £1,000,000 in less than three years; and if the expenses and the revenues should continue the same as in the last two years, there is a probability of an annual deficiency of £300,000. The nation in the last two years has not been able to pay for its own defence: a militia law passed in the last session could not be carried into execution for want of money. Instead of paying forces abroad,[123] Ireland has not been able in this year to pay the forces kept in the kingdom: it has again relapsed into its ancient state of imbecility, and Great Britain has been lately obliged to send over money to pay the army[124] which defends this impoverished country.

Our distress and poverty are of the utmost notoriety; the proof does not depend solely upon calculation or estimate, it is palpable in every public and private transaction, and is deeply felt among all orders of our people.

This kingdom has been long declining. The annual deficiency of its revenues for the payment of the public expenses has been for many years supplied by borrowing. The American rebellion, which considerably diminished the demand for our linens; an embargo on provisions continued for three years,[125] and highly injurious to our victualling trade; the increasing drain of remittances to England for rents, salaries, profits of offices, pensions and interest, and for the payment of forces abroad, have made the decline more rapid, but have not occasioned it.

If we are determined to investigate the truth we must assign a more radical cause; when the human or political body is unsound or infirm it is in vain to inquire what accidental circumstances appear to have occasioned those maladies which arise from the constitution itself.

If in a period of fourscore years of profound internal peace any country shall appear to have often experienced the extremes of poverty and distress; if at the

---

[123] On account of the inability of Ireland, Great Britain, since Christmas, 1778, relieved her from the burden of paying forces abroad.

[124] A sum of £50,000 has been lately sent from England for that purpose.

[125] By a Proclamation, dated the 3rd of February, 1776, on all ships and vessels laden in any of the ports in this kingdom with provisions of any kind, but not to extend to ships carrying salted beef, pork, butter and bacon into Great Britain or provisions to any part of the British empire except the Colonies mentioned in the said Proclamation. 4th of January, 1779, taken off as far as it relates to ships carrying provisions to any of the ports of Europe.

times of her greatest supposed affluence and prosperity the slightest causes have been sufficient to obstruct her progress, to annihilate her credit, and to spread dejection and dismay among all ranks of her people; and if such a country is blessed with a temperate climate and fruitful soil, abounds with excellent harbours and great rivers, with the necessaries of life and materials of manufacture, and is inhabited by a race of men, brave, active, and intelligent, some permanent cause of such disastrous effects must be sought for.

If your vessel is frequently in danger of foundering in the midst of a calm, if by the smallest addition of sail she is near oversetting, let the gale be ever so steady, you would neither reproach the crew nor accuse the pilot or the master; you would look to the construction of the vessel and see how she had been originally framed and whether any new works had been added to her that retard or endanger her course.

But for such an examination more time and attention are necessary than have been usually bestowed upon this subject in Great Britain, and as I have now the honour to address a person of rank and station in that kingdom on the affairs of Ireland I should be brief in my first audience, or I may happen never to obtain the favour of a second.

I have the honour to be, my Lord, &c.

SECOND LETTER.

Dublin, 23rd August, 1779.

My Lord,

If there is any such permanent cause from which the frequent distresses of so considerable a part of the British Empire have arisen, it is of the utmost consequence that it should be fully explained and generally understood. Let us endeavour to trace it by its effects; these will manifestly appear by an attentive review of the state of Ireland at different periods.

From the time that King James the First had established a regular administration of justice in every part of the kingdom, until the rebellion of 1641, which takes in a period of between thirty and forty years, the growth of Ireland was considerable.[126] In the Act recognising the title of King James, the Lords and Commons acknowledge, "that many blessings and benefits had, within these few years past, been poured upon this realm;"[127] and at the end of the Parliament, in 1615, the Commons return thanks for the extraordinary pains taken for the good of this republic, whereby they say: "We all of us sit under our own vines, and the whole realm reapeth the happy fruits of peace."[128] In his reign the little that could be given by the people was given with general consent,[129] and received with extraordinary marks of royal favour. He desires the Lord Deputy to return them thanks for their subsidy, and for their granting it with universal consent,[130] and to assure them that he holds his subjects of that kingdom in equal favour with those of his other kingdoms, and that he will be as careful to provide for their prosperous and flourishing state as for his own person.

Davis, who had served him in great stations in this kingdom, and had visited every province of it, mentions the prosperous state of the country, and that the revenue of the Crown, both certain and casual, had been raised to a double proportion. He takes notice how this was effected "by the encouragement given to the maritime towns and cities, as well to increase the trade of merchandize as to cherish mechanical arts;" and mentions the consequence, "that the strings of this

---

[126] Its tranquillity was so well established in 1611, that King James reduced his army in Ireland to 176 horse and 1,450 foot; additional judges were appointed, circuits established throughout the kingdom (2nd Cox, 17); and Sir John Davis observes that no nation under the sun loves equal and indifferent justice better than the Irish (Davis, pp. 184-196).

[127] 13 Jac., ch. 1.

[128] Vol. i. Com. Journ., p. 92.

[129] Vol. i. Com. Journ., p. 61.

[130] Ib., p. 88.

Irish harp were all in tune."[131]

In the succeeding reign, Ireland, for fourteen or fifteen years, appears to have greatly advanced in prosperity. The Commons granted in the session of 1634 six entire subsidies, which they agreed should amount in the collection to £250,000,[132] and the free gifts previously given to King Charles the First at different times amounted to £310,000.[133] In the session of 1639 they gave four entire subsidies, and the clergy eight; the customs, which had been farmed at £500 yearly in the beginning of this reign, were in the progress of it set for £54,000.[134]

The commodities exported were twice as much in value as the foreign merchandize imported, and shipping is said to have increased an hundred-fold.[135] Their Parliament was encouraged to frame laws conducive to the happiness of themselves and their posterities, for the enacting and "consummating" whereof the king passes his royal word, and assures his subjects of Ireland that they were equally of as much respect and dearness to him as any others.[136]

In the Speaker's speech in 1639, when he was offered for approbation to the Lord Deputy, he mentions the free and happy condition of the people of Ireland, sets forth the particulars, and in enumerating the national blessings, mentions as one "that our in-gates and out-gates do stand open for trade and traffic;"[137] and as the Lord Chancellor declared his Excellency's "high liking of this oration," it may be considered as a fair account of the condition of Ireland at that time. When the Commons had afterwards caught the infection of the times, and were little disposed to pay compliments, they acknowledge that this kingdom, when the Earl of Strafford obtained the government, "was in a flourishing, wealthy, and happy estate."[138]

After the Restoration, from the time that the acts of settlement and explanation had been fully carried into execution to the year 1688, Ireland made great advances, and continued for several years in a most prosperous condition.[139] Lands were everywhere improved; rents were doubled; the kingdom abounded with money; trade flourished to the envy of our neighbours; cities increased exceedingly; many places of the kingdom equalled the improvements of England; the king's revenue increased proportionably to the advance of the kingdom, which was every day

[131] 1 Davis, pp. 1, 193, 194.

[132] Cox's Hist. of Ireland, vol. ii., p. 91.

[133] Ib. Some of these subsidies, from the subsequent times of confusion, were not raised.

[134] Cox, vol. ii., p. 33.

[135] Leland's Hist. of Ireland, vol. iii., p. 31.

[136] Lord Strafford's Letters, vol. ii., p. 297.

[137] Ir. Com. Journ., vol. i., pp. 228-229.

[138] Lord Clarendon, Cox, ib., Ir. Com. Journ., vol. ii., pp. 280, 311.

[139] Archbishop King in his State of the Protestants of Ireland, pp. 52, 53, 445, 446; Lord Chief Justice Keating's Address to James the Second, and his Letters to Sir John Temple. Ib.

The prohibition of the exportation of our cattle to England, though a great, was but a temporary distress; and in its consequences greatly promoted the general welfare of this country.

growing, and was *well established in plenty and wealth;*[140] manufactures were set on foot in divers parts; the meanest inhabitants were at once enriched and civilized; and this kingdom is then represented to be the most improved and improving spot of ground in Europe. I repeat the words of persons of high rank, great character, and superior knowledge, who could not be deceived themselves, and were incapable of deceiving others.

In the former of these periods Parliaments were seldom convened in Ireland; in the latter, they were suspended for the space of twenty-six years; during that time the English ministers frequently showed dispositions unfavourable to the prosperity of this kingdom; and in the interval between those two periods it had been laid waste, and almost depopulated by civil rage and religious fury. And yet, after being blessed with an internal peace of ninety years, and with a succession of five excellent sovereigns, who were most justly the objects of our affection and gratitude, and to whom the people of this country were deservedly dear; after so long and happy an intercourse of protection, grace, and favour from the Crown, and of duty and loyalty from the subjects, it would be difficult to find any subsequent period where so flattering a view has been given of the industry and prosperity of Ireland.

The cause of this prosperity should be mentioned. James, the first Duke of Ormond, whose memory should be ever revered by every friend of Ireland, to heal the wound that this country had received by the prohibition of the export of her cattle to England, obtained from Charles the Second a letter[141] dated the 23rd of March, 1667, by which he directed that all restraints upon the exportation of commodities of the growth or manufacture of Ireland to foreign parts should be taken off, but not to interfere with the plantation laws, or the charters to the trading companies, and that this should be notified to his subjects of this kingdom, which was accordingly done by a proclamation from the Lord Lieutenant and Council; and at the same time, by his Majesty's permission, they prohibited the importation from Scotland of linen, woollen, and other manufactures and commodities, as drawing large sums of money out of Ireland, and a great hindrance to its manufactures. His Grace successfully executed his schemes of national improvement, having by his own constant attention, the exertion of his extensive influence, and the most princely munificence, greatly advanced the woollen and revived[142] the linen manufactures, which England then encouraged in this kingdom as a compensation for the loss of that trade of which she had deprived it, and this encouragement from that time to the Revolution had greatly increased the wealth and promoted the improvement of Ireland.

The tyranny and persecuting policy of James the Second,[143] after his arrival in Ireland, ruined its trade and revenue; the many great oppressions which the people suffered during the revolution had occasioned almost the *utter desolation*

[140] Lord Sydney's words, in his speech from the throne in 1692, from his own former knowledge of this country. Ir. Com. Journ., vol. ii., p. 577.

[141] Carte, vol. ii., pp. 342, 344.

[142] Lord Strafford laid the foundation of the linen manufacture in Ireland, but the troubles which soon after broke out had entirely stopped the progress of it.

[143] Harris's Life of K. W., 116.

of the country.[144] But the nation must have been restored in the reign of William to a considerable degree of strength and vigour; their exertions in raising supplies to a great amount, from the year 1692 to the year 1698, are some proof of it. They taxed their goods, their lands, their persons, in support of a prince whom they justly called their deliverer and defender, and of a government on which their own preservation depended. Those sums were granted,[145] not only without murmur, but with the utmost cheerfulness, and without any complaint of the inability, or representation of the distressed state of the country.

The money brought in for the army at the revolution gave life to all business, and much sooner than could have been expected retrieved the affairs of Ireland. This money furnished capitals for carrying on the manufactures of the kingdom. Our exports increased in '96, '97, and '98, and our imports did not rise in proportion, which occasioned a great balance in our favour; and this increase was owing principally to the woollen manufacture. In the last of those years the balance in favour of Ireland in the account of exports and imports was £419,442.[146]

But in the latter end of this reign the political horizon was overcast, the national growth was checked, and the national vigour and industry impaired by the law made in England restraining, in fact prohibiting, the exportation of all woollen manufactures from Ireland. From the time of this prohibition no parliament was held in Ireland until the year 1703. Five years were suffered to pass before any opportunity was given to apply a remedy to the many evils which such a prohibition must necessarily have occasioned. The linen trade was then not thoroughly established in Ireland; the woollen manufacture was the staple trade, and wool the principal material of that kingdom. The consequences of this prohibition appear in the session of 1703.[147] The Commons[148] lay before Queen Anne a most affecting representation, containing, to use their own words, "a true state of our deplorable condition," protesting that no groundless discontent was the motive for that application, but a deep sense of the evil state of their country, and of the farther mischiefs they have reason to fear will fall upon it if not timely prevented. They set forth the vast decay and loss of its trade, its being almost exhausted of coin, that they are hindered from earning their livelihoods and from maintaining their own manufactures, that their poor have thereby become very numerous; that great numbers of Protestant families have been constrained to remove out of the kingdom, as well into Scotland as into the dominions of foreign princes and states, and that their foreign trade and its returns are under such restrictions and discouragements as to be then become in a manner impracticable, although that kingdom had by its blood and treasure contributed to secure the plantation trade to the people of England.

---

[144] The words of Lord Sydney, in his speech from the throne in 1692. Com. Journ., vol. ii., p. 576.

[145] Ir. Com. Journ., vol. iii., pp. 45 and 65, that great supplies were given during this period.

[146] Dobbs, pp. 5, 6, 7, 19.

[147] Com. Journ., vol. iii., p. 45.

[148] Ir. Com. Journ., vol. iii., pp. 65, 66.

In a further address to the Queen,[149] laid before the Duke of Ormond, then Lord Lieutenant, by the House, with its Speaker, they mention the distressed condition of that kingdom, and more especially of the industrious Protestants, by the almost total loss of trade and decay of their manufactures, and, to preserve the country from utter ruin, apply for liberty to export their linen manufactures to the plantations.

In a subsequent part of this session[150] the Commons resolve that, by reason of the great decay of trade and discouragement of the manufactures of this kingdom, many poor tradesmen were reduced to extreme want and beggary. This resolution was *nem. con.*, and the Speaker, Mr. Broderick, then his Majesty's Solicitor-General, and afterwards Lord Chancellor, in his speech at the end of the session[151] informs the Lord Lieutenant, that the representation of the Commons was, as to the matters contained in it, the unanimous voice and consent of a very full house, and that the soft and gentle terms used by the Commons in laying the distressed condition of the kingdom before his Majesty, showed that their complaints proceeded not from querulousness, but from a necessity of seeking redress, He adds: "It is to be hoped they may be allowed such a proportion of trade that they may recover from the great poverty they now lie under;" and in presenting the bill of supply says, the Commons have granted it "in time of extreme poverty." The impoverished state of Ireland, at that time, appears in the speech from the throne at the conclusion of the session, in which it is mentioned that the Commons could not then provide for what was owing to the civil and military lists.[152]

The supply given for two years, commencing at Michaelmas, 1703,[153] was a sum not exceeding £150,000, which, considering that no Parliament was held in Ireland since the year 1698, is at the rate of £30,000 yearly, commencing in 1699, and ending in the year 1705.

The great distress of Ireland, from the year 1699 to the year 1703, and the cause of that distress, cannot be doubted.

Let it now be considered, whether the same cause has operated since the year 1703. In the year 1704[154] it appears, that the Commons were not able, from the circumstances of the nation at that time, to make provision for repairing the necessary fortifications; or for arms and ammunition for the public safety: and the difficulties which the kingdom then laboured under, and the decay of trade appear by the addresses of the Commons[155] to the Queen, and to the Duke of Ormond, then Lord Lieutenant, who was well acquainted with the state of this country; by the Queen's answer,[156] and the address of thanks for it.

---

[149] Com. Journ., vol. iii., p. 149.

[150] Ib. p. 195.

[151] Ir. Com. Journ., vol. iii., pp. 207, 208.

[152] Com. Journ., vol. iii., p. 210.

[153] Ib., pp. 79, 94.

[154] Com. Journ., vol. iii., p. 298.

[155] Ib., pp. 225, 266.

[156] Ib., pp. 253, 258.

In the year 1707,[157] the revenue was deficient for payment of the army and defraying the charges of government, and the Commons promise to supply the deficiency "as far as the present circumstances of the nation will allow."

In 1709, it appears,[158] by the unanimous address of the Commons to the Lord Lieutenant, that the kingdom was in an impoverished and exhausted state: in 1711,[159] they express their approbation of the frugality of the Queen's administration, by which their expenses were lessened, and by that means the kingdom preserved from taxes, which might have proved too weighty and burdensome. In their address to the Lord Lieutenant at, the close of the session, they request that he should represent to her Majesty, that they had given all the supplies which her Majesty desired, and which they, in their present condition, were able to grant:[160] and yet those supplies amounted, for two years, to a sum not exceeding £167,023 8s. 5d.;[161] though powder magazines, the council chamber, the treasury office, and other offices were then to be built.

From the Short Parliament of 1713, nothing can be collected, but that the House was inflamed and divided by party dissensions, and that the fear of danger to the succession of the present illustrious family, excluded every other consideration from the minds of the majority.

This last period, from the year 1699 to the death of Queen Anne, is marked with the strongest circumstances of national distress and despondency. The representatives of the people, who were the best judges, and several of whom were members of the House of Commons before and after these restraints, have assigned the reason. No other can be assigned.

That the woollen manufactures were the great source of industry in Ireland, appears from the Irish statute of the 17th and 18th of Charles II., ch. 15;[162] from the resolutions of the Commons, in 1695,[163] for regulating those manufactures, the resolutions of the Committee of Supply in that session;[164] and from the preamble to the English statute of the 10th and 11th of William III., ch. 10; in which it is recited, that great quantities of those manufactures were made, and were daily increasing in Ireland, and were exported from thence to foreign markets.

Of the exportation of all those manufactures the Irish were at once totally deprived: the linen manufacture, proposed as a substitute, must have required the attention of many years before it could be thoroughly established. What must have been the consequences to Ireland in the meantime the journals of the Commons in Queen Anne's reign have informed us. Compare this period with the three former,

---

[157] Ib., pp. 364, 368, 369.

[158] Ib., p. 573.

[159] Com. Journ., vol. iii., p. 827.

[160] Ib., p. 929.

[161] Ib., p. 876.

[162] In the same session an act was made for the advancement of the linen manufacture, which shows that both kingdoms then thought (for these laws came to us through England) that each of these manufactures was to be encouraged in Ireland.

[163] Ir. Com. Journ., vol. ii., p. 725.

[164] Ib., p. 733.

and you will prove this melancholy truth: that a country will sooner recover from the miseries and devastation occasioned by war, invasion, rebellion, massacre, than from laws restraining the commerce, discouraging the manufactures, fettering the industry, and above all breaking the spirits of the people.

It would be injustice not to acknowledge that Great Britain has, for a long series of years, made great exertions to repair the evils arising from these restraints. She has opened her great markets to part of the linen manufacture of Ireland; she has encouraged it by granting, for a great length of time, large sums of her own money[165] on the exportation of it; and under her protection, and by the persevering industry of our people, this manufacture has attained to a great degree of perfection and prosperity, in some parts of this country. If the kind and constant attention of that great kingdom with which we are connected, to this important object; or if the lenient course of time had at length healed those wounds, which commercial jealousy had given to the trade and industry of this country, it would not be a friendly hand to either kingdom that would attempt to open them: but, if upon every accident they bleed anew, they should be carefully examined, and searched to the bottom. If the cause of the poverty and distress of Ireland in the reign of Queen Anne has since continued to operate, though not always in so great a degree, yet sufficient frequently to reduce to misery, and constantly to check the growth and impair the strength of that kingdom, and to weaken the force and to reduce the resources of Great Britain; that man ought to be considered as a friend to the British Empire who endeavours to establish this important truth, and to explain a subject so little understood. If in this attempt there shall appear no intention to raise jealousies, inflame discontents, or agitate constitutional questions, it is hoped that those letters may be read without prejudice on one side of the water, and without passion or resentment on the other.

I have the honour to be, my Lord, &c.

---

[165] The sums paid on the exportation of Irish linens from Great Britain, at a medium of twenty-nine years, from 1743 to 1773, amount to something under £10,000 yearly.—Ir. Com. Journ., vol. xvi., p. 374, the account returned from the Inspector-General's Office in Great Britain.

THIRD LETTER.

Dublin, 25th August, 1779.

My Lord,

To an inquirer after truth, history, since the year 1699 furnishes very imperfect and often partial views of the affairs of Great Britain and Ireland. The latter has no professed historian of its own since that era, and is so slightly mentioned in the histories of the former kingdom, that it seems to be introduced rather to show the accuracy of the accomptant, than as an article to be read and examined; pamphlets are often written to serve occasional purposes, and with an intention to misrepresent; and party writers are not worthy of any regard. We must then endeavour to find some other guide, and look into the best materials for history, by considering the facts as recorded in the journals of Parliament; these have evinced the poverty of Ireland for the first fourteen years of this century. That this poverty continued in the year 1716, appears by the unanimous address of the House of Commons to George the First.[166] This address was to congratulate his Majesty on his success in extinguishing the rebellion, an occasion most joyful to them, and on which no disagreeable circumstance would have been stated, had not truth and the necessities of their country extorted it from them. A small debt of £16,106 11s. 0½d.,[167] due at Michaelmas, 1715, was, by their exertions to strengthen the hands of Government in that year, increased at midsummer, 1717, to a sum of £91,537 17s. 1⅝d.,[168] which was considered as such an augmentation of the national debt, that the Lord Lieutenant, the Duke of Bolton, thought it necessary to take notice in his speech from the throne, that the debt was considerably augmented, and to declare at the same time that his Majesty had ordered reductions in the military, and had thought proper to lessen the civil list.

There cannot be a stronger proof of the want of resources in any country, than that a debt of so small an amount should alarm the persons entrusted with the government of it. That those apprehensions were well founded, will appear from the repeated distresses of Ireland, from time to time, for many years afterwards. In 1721, the speech from the throne,[169] and the addresses to the king and to the Lord Lieutenant, state, in the strongest terms, the great decay of her trade, and the very low and impoverished state to which she was reduced.

That this proceeded, in some measure, from calamities and misfortunes which

---

[166] Com. Journ., vol. iv., p. 249.

[167] Ib., p. 296.

[168] Ib., p. 335.

[169] Com. Journ., vol. iv., pp. 694, 700, 701.

affected the neighbouring kingdoms, is true: but their effects on Ireland, little interested in the South Sea project, could not be considerable. The poverty under which she laboured arose principally from her own situation. The Lord Lieutenant says there is ground to hope that in this session such remedies may be applied as will restore the nation to a flourishing condition; and the Commons return the king thanks for giving them that opportunity to consider of the best methods for reviving their decayed trade and making them a flourishing and happy people.

But it is a melancholy proof of the desponding state of this kingdom, that no law whatever was then proposed for encouraging trade or manufactures, or to follow the words of the address, for reviving trade, or making us a flourishing people, unless that for amending the laws as to butter and tallow casks deserves to be so called. And why? Because it was well understood by both Houses of Parliament that they had no power to remove those restraints which prohibited trade and discouraged manufactures, and that any application for that purpose would at that time have only offended the people on one side of the channel without bringing any relief to those on the other. The remedy proposed by Government, and partly executed, by directing a commission under the Great Seal for receiving voluntary subscriptions[170] in order to establish a bank, was a scheme to circulate paper without money; and considering that it came so soon after the South Sea Bubble had burst, it is more surprising that it should have been at first applauded,[171] than that it was, in the same session, disliked, censured, and abandoned.[172] The total inefficacy of the remedy proved however the inveteracy of the disease, and furnishes a farther proof of the desperate situation of Ireland, when nothing could be thought of for its relief, but that paper should circulate without money, trade, or manufactures.[173]

In the following session of 1723, it appears that the condition of our manufacturers, and of the lowest classes of our people, must have been distressed, as the Duke of Grafton, in his speech from the throne, particularly recommends to their consideration the finding out of some method for the better employing of the poor;[174] and though the debt of the nation was no more than £66,318 8s. 3¼d.,[175] and was less than in the *last* session,[176] yet the Commons thought it necessary to present an address to the king, to give such directions as he, in his great goodness, should think proper, to prevent the increase of the debt of the nation. This address was presented[177] by the House, with its Speaker, and passed *nem. con.*, and was occasioned by the distressed state of the country, and by their apprehensions that it might be further exhausted by the project of Wood's halfpence: it could not be meant as any want of respect to their Lord Lieutenant, as they had not long since

---

[170] Ir. Com. Journ., vol. iv., p. 694.

[171] Ib., p. 720.

[172] Ib., p. 832.

[173] It is not here intended to enter into the question, whether in different circumstances a national bank might not be useful to Ireland.

[174] Com. Journ., vol. v., p. 12.

[175] Ib., p. 102.

[176] It was then £77,261 6s. 7d. Vol. iv., p. 778.

[177] Com. Journ., vol. iv., p. 108.

returned him thanks for his wise conduct and frugality in not increasing the debt of the nation.[178] This address of the Commons, and the Lord Lieutenant's recommendation for the better employing the poor, seems to be explained by a petition of the woollen drapers, weavers, and clothiers of the city of Dublin (the principal seat of the woollen manufacture of Ireland) in behalf of themselves and the other drapers, weavers, and clothiers of this kingdom, praying relief in relation to the great decay of trade in the woollen manufacture.[179]

But this address had no effect; the debt of the nation in the ensuing session of 1725, was nearly doubled.[180] In the speeches from the throne, in 1727, Lord Carteret takes notice of our success in the linen trade, and yet observes, in 1729, that the revenue had fallen short, and that thereby a considerable arrear was due to the establishment.

But notwithstanding the success of the linen manufacture,[181] Ireland was in a most miserable condition. The great scarcity of corn had been so universal in this kingdom in the years 1728 and 1729, as to expose thousands of families to the utmost necessities, and even to the danger of famine; many artificers and housekeepers having been obliged to beg for bread in the streets of Dublin. It appeared before the House of Commons that the import of corn for one year and six months, ending the 29th day of September, 1729, amounted in value to the sum of £274,000, an amazing sum compared with the circumstances of the kingdom at that time! and the Commons resolved that public granaries would greatly contribute to the increasing of tillage, and providing against such wants as have frequently befallen the people of this kingdom, and hereafter may befall them, unless proper precautions shall be taken against so great a calamity.

The great scarcity which happened in the years '28 and '29, and frequently before and since, is a decisive proof that the distresses of this kingdom have been occasioned by the discouragement of manufactures. If the manufacturers have not sufficient employment, they cannot buy the superfluous produce of the land; the farmers will be discouraged from tilling, and general distress and poverty must ensue. The consequences of the want of employment among manufacturers and labourers must be more fatal in Ireland than in most other countries; of the numbers of her people it has been computed that 1,887,220 live in houses with but one hearth, and may therefore be reasonably presumed to belong for the most part to those classes.

In the year 1731[182] there was a great deficiency in the public revenue, and the national debt had considerably increased. The exhausted kingdom lay under great difficulties by the decay of trade, the scarcity of money, and the universal poverty of the country, which the Speaker represents[183] in very affecting terms, in

---

[178] Ib., p. 16.

[179] Com. Journ., vol. iv., p. 136.

[180] At midsummer, 1725, it amounted to £119,215 5s. 3⅝d. Vol. v., Com. Journ., pp. 282, 295, 434, 435, 642.

[181] Com. Journ., vol. v., pp. 732, 755.

[182] Duke of Dorset's speech from the throne. Com. Journ., vol. vi., p. 12.

[183] Com. Journ., vol. vi., p. 143.

offering the money bills for the royal assent, and adds, "that the Commons hope, from his Majesty's goodness, and his Grace's *free* and *impartial* representation of the state and condition of this kingdom, that *they* may enjoy a *share* of the blessings of public tranquillity by the increase of their trade, and the encouragement of their manufactures."

But in the next session, of 1733, they are told in the speech from the throne, what this share was to be. The Lord Lieutenant informs them that the peace cannot fail of contributing to their welfare, by enabling them to improve those branches of trade and manufactures[184] which *are properly their own*, meaning the trade and manufacture of linen. Whether this idea of property has been preserved inviolate will hereafter appear.

The years '40 and '41 were seasons of great scarcity, and in consequence of the want of wholesome provisions great numbers of our people perished miserably, and the speech from the throne recommends it to both Houses to consider of proper measures to prevent the like calamity for the future. The employment of the poor and the encouragement of tillage are the remedies proposed[185] by the Lord Lieutenant and approved of by the Commons, but no laws for those purposes were introduced, and why they were not affords matter for melancholy conjecture. They could not have been insensible of the miseries of their fellow-creatures, many thousands of whom were lost in those years, some from absolute want, and many from disorders occasioned by bad provisions. Why was no attempt made for their relief? Because the Commons knew that the evil was out of their reach, that the poor were not employed because they were discouraged by restrictive laws from working up the materials of their own country, and that agriculture could not be encouraged where the lower classes of the people were not enabled by their industry to purchase the produce of the farmer's labour.

For above forty years after making those restrictive laws[186] Ireland was always poor and often in great want, distress, and misery,[187] though the linen manufacture had made great progress during that time. In the war before the last, she was not able to give any assistance. The Duke of Devonshire, in the year 1741, takes notice from the throne, that during a war for the protection of the trade of all his Majesty's dominions there had been no increase of the charge of the establishment; and in the year 1745, the country was so little able to bear expense, that lord Chesterfield discouraged and prevented any augmentation of the army, though much desired by many gentlemen of the House of Commons, from a sense of the great danger that then impended. An influx of money after the peace, and the further success of the linen trade, increased our wealth, and enabled us to reduce by degrees, and afterwards to discharge the national debt. This was not effected until the first of March, 1754.[188] This debt was occasioned principally by the ex-

[184] Ib., vol. vi., p. 189.

[185] Com. Journ., vol. v., pp. 214, 220, 222.

[186] The act entitled an act for better regulation of partnerships and to encourage the trade and manufactures of this kingdom has not a word relative to the latter part of the title.

[187] Com. Journ., vol. vi., p. 694; ib., vol. vii., p. 742.

[188] The sum remaining due on the loans at Lady-day, 1753, was £85,585 0s. 9½d. The whole credit of the nation to that day was £332,747 19s. 1⅛d., and deducting the sums due

penses incurred by the rebellion in Great Britain in the year 1715; an unlimited vote of credit was then given.[189] From the lowness of the revenue, and the want of resources, not from any further exertions on the part of the kingdom in point of expense, the debt of £16,106 11s. 0½d., due in 1715, was increased at Lady-day,[190] 1733, to £371,312 12s. 2½d. That Government and the House of Commons should for such a length of time have considered the reduction and discharge of this debt as an object of so great importance, and that nearly forty years should have passed before the constant attention and strictest economy of both could have accomplished that purpose, is a strong proof of the weakness and poverty of this country, during that period.

After the payment of this debt, the wealth and ability of Ireland were greatly overrated, both here and in Great Britain. The consequences of this mistaken opinion were increased expenses on the part of government and of the country, more than it was able to bear. The strict economy of old times was no longer practised. The representatives of the people set the example of profusion and the ministers of the Crown were not backward in following it. A large redundancy of money in the Treasury, gave a delusive appearance of national wealth. At Lady-day, 1755, the sum in credit to the nation was £471,404 5s. 6⅜d.,[191] and the money remaining in the Treasury of the ordinary unappropriated revenue on the 29th day of September, 1755,[192] £457,959 12s. 7⅛d. But this great increase of revenue arose from an increase of imports, particularly in the year 1754, by which the kingdom was greatly over-stocked, and which raised the revenue in that year £208,309 19s. 2¼d. higher than it was in the year 1748, when the revenue first began to rise considerably;[193] and though what a nation spends is one method of estimating its wealth, yet a nation, like an individual, may live beyond its means, and spend on credit which may far exceed its income. This was the fact as to Ireland in the year 1754, for some years before and for many years after; it appeared in an inquiry before the House of Commons in the session of 1755, that many persons had circulated paper to a very great amount, far exceeding not only their own capitals,[194] but that just proportion which the quantity of paper ought to bear to the national specie.[195] This gave credit to many individuals, who without property became merchant importers, and at the same time increased the receipts of the Treasury and lessened the wealth of the kingdom. At the very time that so great a balance was in the Treasury, public credit was in a very low way, and the House of Commons was employed in preparing a law to restore it. In '54 and '55 three principal banks[196] failed, and the legislature took up much time in inquiring into their affairs, and

---

on the loans amounted to £247,162 18s. 3⅛d. Com. Journ., vol. ix. pp. 3, 349, 352.

[189] Com. Journ., vol. iv., p. 195.

[190] Com. Journ., vol. vi., p. 289.

[191] Ib., vol. ix., p. 352.

[192] Ib., p. 332.

[193] Com. Journ., vol. x., p. 751.

[194] Ib., vol. ix., p. 818.

[195] Ib., pp. 819, 829, 846, 865.

[196] March 6, 1754, Thomas Dillon and Richard Ferral, failed. 3rd March, 1755, William Lennox and George French. Same day, John Wilcocks and John Dawson.

in framing laws for the relief of their creditors.[197] Yet in this session, the liberality of the House of Commons was excessive. The redundancy in the Treasury had, in the session of 1753, occasioned a dispute between the Crown and the House of Commons on the question whether the king's previous consent was necessary for the application of it. They wished to avoid any future contest of that kind, and were flattered to grant the public money from enlarged views of national improvements. The making rivers navigable, the making and improving harbours, and the improvement of husbandry and other useful arts, were objects worthy of the representatives of the people; and had the faithfulness of the execution answered the goodness of the intention in many instances, the public in general might have had no great reason to complain. Many of those grants prove the poverty of the country. There were not private stocks to carry on the projects of individuals, nor funds sufficient for incorporating and supporting companies, nor profits to be had by the undertakings sufficient to reimburse the money necessary to be expended. The Commons therefore advanced the money, for the benefit of the public; and it can never be supposed that they would have continued to do so for above twenty years, if they were not convinced that there were not funds in the hands of individuals sufficient to carry on those useful undertakings, nor trade enough in the kingdom to make adequate returns to the adventurers.

Having gone through more than half the century, it is time to pause. In this long gloomy period, the poverty of Ireland appears to have been misery and desolation, and her wealth a symptom of decline and a prelude to poverty; the low retiring ebb from the spring-tide of deceitful prosperity, has left our shores bare, and has opened a waste and desolate prospect of barren sand, and uncultivated country.

I have the honour to be, my Lord, &c.

---

[197] There was then no bankruptcy law in Ireland.

FOURTH LETTER.

Dublin, 27th August, 1779.

My Lord,

The revenue, for the reasons already given, decreased in 1755,[198] fell lower in 1756, and still lower in '57. In the last year the vaunted prosperity of Ireland was changed into misery and distress; the lower classes of our people wanted food;[199] the money arising from the extravagance of the rich was freely applied to alleviate the sufferings of the poor.[200] One of the first steps of the late Duke of Bedford's administration—and which reflects honour on his memory—was obtaining a king's letter, dated 31st March, 1757, for £20,000, to be laid out as his Grace should think the most likely to afford the most speedy and effectual relief to his Majesty's poor subjects of this kingdom. His Grace, in his speech from the throne, humanely expresses his wish, that some method might be found out to prevent the calamities that are the consequences of a want of corn, which had been in part felt the last year, and to which this country had been too often exposed; the Commons acknowledge that those calamities had been frequently and were too sensibly and fatally experienced in the course of the last year, thank his Grace for his early and charitable attention to the necessities of the poor of this country in their late distresses, and make use of those remarkable expressions, — "that they will most cheerfully embrace[201] every *practicable* method to promote tillage."[202] They knew that the encouragement of manufactures were the effectual means, and that these means were not in their power.

The ability of the nation was estimated by the money in the Treasury, and the pensions on the civil establishment, exclusive of French, which at Lady-Day, 1755, were £38,003 15s., amounted at Lady-Day, '57, to £49,293 15s.[203]

The same ideas were entertained of the resources of this country in the session of 1759. Great Britain had made extraordinary efforts, and engaged in enormous expenses for the protection of the whole empire. This country was in immediate

---

[198] Com. Journ., vol. x., p. 751.

[199] Ib., p. 16, speech from the throne, and ib., p. 25, address from the House of Commons to the king.

[200] Ib., p. 25. Address from the House of Commons to the king.

[201] Com. Journ., vol. x., p. 25.

[202] They brought in a law for the encouragement of tillage, which was ineffectual (see post 42); but the preamble of that Act is a legislative proof of the unhappy condition of the poor of this country before that time. The preamble recites, "the *extreme* necessity to which the poor of this kingdom had been too frequently reduced for want of provisions."

[203] Com. Journ., vol. x., p. 285.

danger of an invasion. Every Irishman was agreed that she should assist Great Britain to the utmost of her ability, but this ability was too highly estimated. The nation abounded rather in loyalty than in wealth.[204] Our brethren in Great Britain, had, however, formed a different opinion, and, surveying their own strength, were incomplete judges of our weakness. A Lord Lieutenant of too much virtue and magnanimity to speak what he did not think, takes notice from the throne, "of the prosperous state of this country, improving daily in its manufactures and commerce."[205] His Grace had done much to bring it to that state, by obtaining for us some of the best laws[206] in our books of statutes. But this part of the speech was not taken notice of, either in the address to his Majesty or to his Grace, from a House of Commons well disposed to give every mark of duty and respect, and to pay every compliment consistent with truth. The event proved the wisdom of their reserve. The public expenses were greatly increased, the pensions on the civil establishment exclusive of French, at Lady-Day, 1759, amounted to £55,497 5s.;[207] there was, at the same time a great augmentation of military expense.[208] Six new regiments and a troop were raised in a very short space of time. An unanimous and unlimited address of confidence to his Grace,[209] a specific vote of credit for £150,000,[210] which was afterwards provided for in the Loan Bill[211] of that session, a second vote of credit in the same session for £300,000,[212] the raising the rate of interest paid by Government, one per cent., and the payment out of the Treasury[213] in little more than one year of £703,957 3s. 1½d.,[214] were the consequences of those increased expenses. The effects of these exertions were immediately and severely felt by the kingdom. These loans could not be supplied by a poor country, without draining the bankers of their cash; three of the principal houses,[215] among them stopped payment; the three remaining banks in Dublin discounted no paper, and, in fact, did no business. Public and private credit, that had been drooping since the year 1754, had now fallen prostrate. At a general meeting of the merchants of Dublin, in April, 1860, with several members of the House of Commons, the inability of the former to carry on business was universally acknowledged, not from the want of capital, but from the stoppage of all paper circulation, and the refusal of the remaining bankers to discount the bills even of the first houses. The merchants and traders of Dublin, in their petition[216] to the House of Commons, represent "the low state to which public and private credit had been of late reduced in this

[204] Com. Journ. vol. xi., p. 472. Speaker's speech.

[205] Ib., p. 16.

[206] The Acts passed in '58, giving bounties on the land carriage of corn, and on coals brought to Dublin.

[207] Com. Journ., vol. xi., p. 212.

[208] Ib., from 826 to 837.

[209] Ib., vol. xi., p. 141.

[210] Ib., p. 408.

[211] Ib., p. 473.

[212] Ib., p. 862.

[213] Ib.

[214] Ib., p. 982, from 25th March, '59, to 21st of April, '60, exclusive.

[215] Clement's, Dawson's, and Mitchell's.

[216] Com. Journ., vol. xi., p. 966, April 15, 1760.

kingdom, and particularly in this city, of which the successive failures of so many banks, and of private traders in different parts of this kingdom, in so short a time as since October last, were incontestable proofs. The petitioners, sensible that the necessary consequences of these misfortunes must be the loss of foreign trade, the diminution of his Majesty's revenue, and what is still more fatal, the decay of the manufactures of this kingdom, have in vain repeatedly attempted to support the sinking credit of the nation by associations and otherwise; and are satisfied that no resource is now left but what may be expected from the wisdom of parliament, to avert the calamities with which this kingdom is at present threatened."

The committee, to whom it was referred, resolve[217] that they had proved the several matters alleged in their petition; that the quantity of paper circulating was not near sufficient for supporting the trade and manufactures of this kingdom; and that the house should engage, to the first of May, '62, for each of the then subsisting banks in Dublin, to the amount of £50,000 for each bank; and that an address should be presented to the Lord Lieutenant, to thank his Grace for having given directions that bankers' notes should be received as cash from the several subscribers to the loan, and that he would be pleased to give directions that their notes should be taken as cash in all payments at the Treasury, and by the several collectors for the city and county of Dublin. The house agreed to those resolutions and to that for giving credit to the banks, *nem. con.*

The speech from the throne takes notice of the care the House of Commons had taken for establishing public credit, which the Lord Lieutenant says he flatters himself will answer the end proposed, and effect that circulation so necessary for carrying on the commerce of the country.[218]

Those facts are not stated as any imputation on the then chief governor: the vigour of his mind incited him to make the Crown as useful as possible to the subject, and the subject to the Crown. He succeeded in both, but in the latter part of the experiment, the weakness of the country was shown. The great law which we owe to his interposition, I speak of that which gives a bounty on the land carriage of corn and flour to Dublin,[219] has saved this country from utter destruction; this law, which reflects the highest honour on the author and promoter, is still a proof of the poverty of that country where such a law is necessary. Its true principle is to bring the market of Dublin to the door of the farmer, and that was done in the year ending the 25th of March, 1777, at the expense of £61,789 18s. 6d., to the public; a large but a most useful and necessary expenditure.[220] The adoption of this principle proves, what we in this country know to be a certain truth, that there is no other market in Ireland on which the farmer can rely for the certain sale of his corn and flour; a decisive circumstance to show the wretched state of the manufactures of this kingdom.

In the beginning of the next parliament the rupture with Spain occasioned a

---

[217] Com. Journ., vol. xi., pp. 993, 994.

[218] Ib., p. 1049.

[219] Brought in by Mr. Pery the present Speaker.

[220] In the year ending Lady-Day, 1778, it amounted to £71,533 1s., and in that ending Lady-Day, 1779, to £67,864 8s. 10d.

new augmentation of military expense. The ever loyal Commons return an address of thanks to the message mentioning the addition of five new battalions[221] and unanimously promise to provide for them; and with the same unanimity pass a vote of credit for £200,000.[222] The amount of pensions on the civil establishment, exclusive of French, had for one year ending the 25th of March, 1761, amounted to £64,127 5s.,[223] and our manufacturers were then distressed by the expense and havoc of a burdensome war.[224]

In the year 1762 a national evil made its appearance, which all the exertions of the Government and of the legislature have not since been able to eradicate; I mean the risings of the White Boys. They appear in those parts of the kingdom where manufactures are not established, and are a proof of the poverty and want of employment of the lower classes of our people. Lord Northumberland mentions, in his speech from the throne[225] in 1763, that the means of industry would be the remedy; from whence it seems to follow that the want of those means must be the cause. To attain this great end the Commons promise their attention to the Protestant charter schools and linen manufacture.[226] The wretched men who were guilty of those violations of the law, were too mature for the first, and totally ignorant of the second; but long established usage had given those words a privilege in speeches and addresses to stand for everything that related to the improvement of Ireland.

The state of pensions remained nearly the same[227] by the peace the military expenses were considerably reduced; of the military establishment to be provided for in the session 1763, compared with the military establishment as it stood on the 31st of March, 1763, the net decrease was £119,037 0s. 10d. per annum; but as a peace establishment it was high, and compared with that of the 31st of March, 1756[228] being the year preceding the last war, the annual increase was £110,422 9s. 5¼d. The debt of the nation at Lady Day, 1763, and which was entirely incurred in the last war, was £521,161 16s. 6⅞d.,[229] and would have been much greater if the several Lord Lieutenants had not used with great economy the power of borrowing, which the House of Commons had from session to session given them.

That this debt should have been contracted in an expensive war, in which Ireland was called upon for the first time to contribute, is not to be wondered at, but the continual increase of this debt, in sixteen years of peace, should be accounted for.

The same mistaken estimate of the ability of Ireland that occasioned our being

[221] Com. Journ., vol. xii, p. 700.

[222] Ib. p. 728.

[223] Ib., p. 443.

[224] Ib. p. 929. Speech of Lord Hallifax from the throne, 30th April, 1762.

[225] Ir. Com. Journ., vol. xiii., p. 21.

[226] Com. Journ., vol. xiii., p. 23.

[227] For a year ending 25th March, 1763, they were £66,477 5s.; they afterwards rose to £89,095 17s. 6d. in September, 1777, at the highest; and in this year, ending the 25th March last, amounted to £85,971 2s. 6d.

[228] Com. Journ. vol. xiii., p. 576.

[229] Ib. pp. 574, 621.

called upon to bear part of the British burden during the war, produced similar effects at the time of the peace, and after it. The heavy peace establishment was increased by an augmentation of our army in 1769, which induced an additional charge, taking in the expenses of exchange and remittance of £54,118 12s. 6d. yearly, for the first year; but this charge was afterwards considerably increased, and amounted, from the year 1769 to Christmas, 1778, when it was discontinued, to the sum of £620,824 0s. 9¼d., and this increased expense was more felt, because it was for the purpose of paying forces out of this kingdom.

As our expenses increased our income diminished; the revenue for the two years, ending the 25th of March, 1771,[230] was far short of former years, and not nearly sufficient to pay the charges of Government, and the sums payable for bounties and public works.[231] The debt of the nation at Lady-Day, 1771, was increased to £782,320 0s. 0¼d.[232] The want of income was endeavoured to be supplied by a loan. In the money bill of the October Session, 1771, there was a clause empowering Government to borrow £200,000. Immediately after the linen trade declined rapidly; in 1772, 1773, and 1774, the decay in that trade was general in every part of the kingdom where it was established; the quantity manufactured was not above two-thirds of what used formerly to be made, and that quantity did not sell for above three-fourths of its former price. The linen and linen yarn exported for one year, ending the 25th of March, 1773,[233] fell short of the exports of one year, ending the 25th of March, 1771, to the amount in value of £788,821 1s. 3d. At Lady-day, 1773,[234] the debt increased to £994,890 10s. 10⅛d. The attempt in the Session of 1773,[235] to equalise the annual income and expenses failed, and borrowing on tontine in the Sessions of 1773, 1775, and 1777, added greatly to the annual expense, and to the sums of money remitted out of the kingdom. The debt now bearing interest amounts to the sum of £1,017,600, besides a sum of £740,000 raised on annuities, which amount to £48,900 yearly, with some incidental expenses. The great increase of those national burdens, likely to take place in the approaching Session, has been already mentioned.

The debt of Ireland has arisen from the following causes: the expenses of the late war, the heavy peace establishment in the year 1763, the increase of that establishment in the year 1769, the sums paid from 1759 to forces out of the kingdom, the great increase of pensions and other additional charges on the civil establishment, which, however considerable, bears but a small proportion to the increased military expenses, the falling of the revenue, and the sums paid for bounties and public works; these are mentioned last, because it is apprehended that they have not operated to increase this debt in so great a degree as some persons have imagined; for, though the amount is large, yet no part of the money was sent out of the kingdom, and several of the grants were for useful purposes, some of which made returns to the public and to the Treasury exceeding the amount of those grants.

[230] Com. Journ., vol. xiv., p. 715.
[231] Com. Journ., vol. xv., p. 710.
[232] Ib., p. 153.
[233] Ib., vol. xvi., p. 372.
[234] Ib., pp. 190, 191, 193.
[235] Ib., p. 256.

When those facts are considered, no doubt can be entertained but that the supposed wealth of Ireland has led to real poverty; and when it is known, that from the year 1751 to Christmas, 1778, the sums remitted by Ireland to pay troops serving abroad, amounted to the sum of £1,401,925 19s. 4d., it will be equally clear from whence this poverty has principally arisen.

In those seasons of expense and borrowing the lower classes were equally subject to poverty and distress, as in the period of national economy. In 1762, Lord Halifax, in his speech from the throne,[236] acknowledges that our manufactures were distressed by the war. In 1763, the corporation of weavers, by a petition to the House of Commons, complain that, notwithstanding the great increase both in number and wealth of the inhabitants of the metropolis, they found a very great decay of several branches of trade and manufactures[237] of this city, particularly in the silken and woollen.

In 1765 there was a scarcity caused by the failure of potatoes in general throughout the kingdom, which distressed the common people; the spring corn had also failed, and grain was so high, that it was thought necessary to appoint a committee[238] to inquire what may be the best method to reduce it; and to prevent a great dearth, two acts were passed early in that session, to stop the distillery, and to prevent the exportation of corn, for a limited time. In Spring, 1766, those fears appear to have been well-founded; several towns were in great distress for corn; and by the humanity of the Lord Lieutenant, Lord Hertford, money was issued out of the Treasury to buy corn for such places as applied to his lordship for that relief.

The years 1770 and 1771 were seasons of great distress in Ireland, and in the month of February, in the latter year, the high price of corn is mentioned from the throne[239] as an object of the first importance, which demanded the utmost attention.

In 1778 and 1779 there was great plenty of corn, but the manufacturers were not able to buy, and many thousands of them were supported by charity; the consequence was that corn fell to so low a price that the farmers in many places were unable to pay their rents, and everywhere were under great difficulties.

That the linen manufacture has been of the utmost consequence to this country, that it has greatly prospered, that it has been long encouraged by the protection of Great Britain, that whatever wealth Ireland is possessed of arises, for the most part, from that trade, is freely acknowledged; but in far the greatest part of the kingdom it has not yet been established, and many attempts to introduce it have, after long perseverance and great expense, proved fruitless.

Though that manufacture made great advances from 1727 to 1758,[240] yet the tillage of this kingdom declined during the whole of that period, and we have not since been free from scarcity.

[236] Com. Journ., vol. xii., p. 928.
[237] Ib., vol. xiii., p. 987.
[238] Ib., vol. xiv., pp. 69, 114, 151.
[239] Com. Journ., vol. xiv., p. 665.
[240] Com. Journ., vol. xiv., p. 467, report from committee, and ib., p. 501, agreed to by the House, *nem. con.*

Notwithstanding the success of that manufacture, the bulk of our people have always continued poor, and in a great many seasons have wanted food. Can the history of any other fruitful country on the globe, enjoying peace for fourscore years, and not visited by plague or pestilence, produce so many recorded instances of the poverty and wretchedness, and of the reiterated want and misery of the lower orders of the people? There is no such example in ancient or modern story. If the ineffectual endeavours by the representatives of those poor people to give them employment and food, had not left sufficient memorials of their wretchedness; if their habitations, apparel, and food, were not sufficient proofs, I should appeal to the human countenance for my voucher, and rest the evidence on that hopeless despondency that hangs on the brow of unemployed industry.

That, since the success of the linen manufacture, the money and the rents of Ireland have been greatly increased, is acknowledged; but it is affirmed, and the fact is of notoriety, that the lower orders, not of that trade, are not less wretched. Those employed in the favourite manufacture generally buy from that country to which they principally sell; and the rise in lands is a misfortune to the poor, where their wages do not rise proportionably, which will not happen where manufactures and agriculture are not sufficiently encouraged. Give premiums by land or by water, arrange your exports and imports in what manner you will; if you discourage the people from working up the principal materials of their country, the bulk of that people must ever continue miserable, the growth of the nation will be checked, and the sinews of the State enfeebled.

I have stated a tedious detail of instances, to show that the sufferings of the lower classes of our people have continued the same (with an exception only of those employed in the linen trade) since the time of Queen Anne, as they were during her reign; that the cause remains the same, namely, that our manufacturers have not sufficient employment, and cannot afford to buy from the farmer, and that therefore manufactures and agriculture must both be prejudiced.

After revolving those repeated instances, and almost continued chain of distress, for such a series of years, among the inhabitants of a temperate climate, surrounded by the bounties of Providence and the means of abundance, and being unable to discover any accidental or natural causes for those evils, we are led to inquire whether they have arisen from the mistaken policy of man.

I have the honour to be, my Lord, &c.

FIFTH LETTER.

Dublin, 30th Aug., 1779.

My Lord,

Every man of discernment, who attends to the facts which have been stated, would conclude, that there must be some political institutions in this country counteracting the natural course of things, and obstructing the prosperity of the people. Those institutions should be considered, that as from the effects the cause has been traced, this also should be examined, to show that such consequences are necessarily deducible from it. For several years the exportation of live cattle to England[241] was the principal trade of Ireland. This was thought, most erroneously,[242] as has since been acknowledged,[243] to lower the rents of lands in England. From this, and perhaps from some less worthy motive[244] a law passed in England,[245] to restrain and afterwards to prohibit the exportation of cattle from Ireland. The Irish, deprived of their principal trade, and reduced to the utmost distress by this prohibition, had no resource but to work up their own commodities, to which they applied themselves with great ardour.[246] After this prohibition they increased their number of sheep, and at the Revolution were possessed of very numerous flocks. They had good reasons to think that this object of industry was not only left open, but recommended to them. The ineffectual attempt by Lord Strafford, in 1639, to prevent the making of broadcloths in Ireland,[247] the relinquishment of that scheme by never afterwards reviving it, the encouragement given to their woollen manufactures by many English Acts of Parliament from the reign of Edward III.[248] to the 12th of Charles II., and several of them for the express purpose of exportation; the letter of Charles II., in 1667, with the advice of his Privy Council in England, and the proclamation in pursuance of that letter, encouraging the exportation of their manufactures to foreign countries; by the Irish statutes of the 13th Henry VIII. ch. 2; 28th Henry VIII. ch. 17; of the 11th Elizabeth, ch. 10, and 17th and 18th Charles II., ch. 15 (all of which, the Act of 28th Henry VIII. excepted, received the approbation of the Privy Council of England, having been returned under the Great Seal of that kingdom) afforded as strong grounds of assurance as

[241] Carte, vol. ii., pp. 318, 319.

[242] Sir W. Petty's "Political Survey," pp. 69, 70. Sir W. Temple, vol. iii., pp. 22, 23.

[243] By several British acts (32 G. 2, ch. 11; 5 G. 3, ch. 10; 12 G. 3, ch. 56), allowing from time to time the free importation of all sorts of cattle from Ireland.

[244] Personal prejudice against the Duke of Ormond (Carte, vol. ii., pp. 332, 337.)

[245] 15 Ch. 2, ch. 7. 18 Ch. 2, ch. 2.

[246] Carte, vol. ii., p. 332.

[247] Com. Journ., vol. i., p. 208, by a clause to be inserted in an Irish act.

[248] See post, those acts stated.

any country could possess for the continuance of any trade or manufacture.

Great numbers of their flocks had been destroyed at the time of the Revolution, but they were replaced, at great expense, and became more numerous and flourishing than before. The woollen manufacture was cultivated in Ireland for ages before, and for several years after the Revolution, without any appearance of jealousy from England, the attempt by Lord Strafford excepted. No discouragement is intimated in any speech from the throne until the year 1698; Lord Sydney's, in 1692, imparts the contrary. "Their Majesties," says he,[249] "being in their own royal judgments satisfied that a country so fertile by nature, and so advantageously situated for *trade and navigation*, can want nothing but the blessing of peace, and the help of some good laws to make it as rich and flourishing *as most of its neighbours*; I am ordered to assure you that nothing shall be wanting on their parts that may contribute to your perfect and lasting happiness."

Several laws had been made[250] in England to prevent the exportation of wool, yarn made of wool, fuller's earth, or any kind of scouring earth or fulling clay from England or Ireland, into any places out of the kingdoms of England or Ireland. But those laws were equally restrictive on both kingdoms.

In the first year[251] of William and Mary certain ports were mentioned in Ireland, from which only wool should be shipped from that kingdom, and certain ports in England into which only it should be imported; and a register was directed to be kept in the Custom House of London of all the wool from time to time imported from Ireland. By a subsequent Act in this reign,[252] passed in 1696, the Commissioners or Farmers of the Customs in Ireland are directed, once in every six months, to transmit to the Commissioners of Customs in England, an account of all wool exported from Ireland to England, and this last Act, in its title, professes the intention of encouraging the importation of wool from Ireland. The prohibition of exporting the materials from either kingdom, except to the other, and the encouragement to export it from Ireland to England, mentioned in the title of the last-mentioned Act, but for which no provision seems to be made, unless the designation of particular ports may be so called, was the system that then seemed to be settled, for preventing the wool of Ireland from being prejudicial to England; but the prevention of the exportation of the manufacture was an idea that seemed never to have been entertained until the year 1697, when a bill for that purpose was brought into the English House of Commons,[253] and passed that house; but after great consideration was not passed by the Lords in that parliament.[254] There does not appear to have been any increase at that time in the woollen manufacture of Ireland sufficient to have raised any jealousy in England.

By a report from the Commissioners of Trade in that kingdom, dated on the 23rd of December, 1697, and laid before the House of Commons, in 1698, they

[249] Com. Journ., vol. ii., p. 576.
[250] English acts, 12 Ch. 2, ch. 32, 13 and 14. Ch. 2, ch. 18.
[251] 1 W., and M. ch. 32.
[252] 7 and 8 W., ch. 28.
[253] 14th Jan., 1697.
[254] 7th July, 1698, dissolved.

find that the woollen manufacture in Ireland had increased since the year 1665, as follows:

Years.	New draperies. Pieces.	Old draperies. Pieces.	Frieze. Yards.
1665	224	32	444,381
1687	11,360	103	1,129,716
1696	4,413	34¾	104,167

The bill for restraining the exportation of woollen manufactures from Ireland was brought into the English House of Commons on the 23rd of February, 1697, but the law did not pass until the year 1699, in the first session of the new parliament. I have not been able to obtain an account of the exportation of woollen manufactures for the year 1697,[255] but from the 25th of December, 1697, to the 25th of December, 1698, being the first year in which the exports in books extant are registered in the Custom House at Dublin, the amount appears to be of

New draperies. Pieces.	Old draperies. Pieces.	Frieze. Yards.
23,285½	281½	666,901

though this increase of export shows that the trade was advancing in Ireland, yet the total amount or the comparative increase since 1687 could scarcely "sink the value of lands and tend to the ruin of the trade and woollen manufactures of England."[256]

The apprehensions of England seem rather to have arisen from the fears of future, than from the experience of any past rivalship in this trade. I have more than once heard Lord Bowes, the late chancellor of this kingdom, mention a conversation that he had with Sir Robert Walpole on this subject, who assured him that the jealousies entertained in England of the woollen trade in Ireland, and the restraints of that trade had at first taken their rise from the boasts of some of our countrymen in London, of the great success of that manufacture here. Whatever was the cause, both houses of parliament in England addressed King William, in very strong terms, on this subject; but on considering those addresses they seem to be founded, not on the state at that time of that manufacture here, but the probability of its further increase. As those proceedings are of great importance to two of the principal manufactures of this country, it is thought necessary to state them particularly. The lords represent, "that the *growing* manufacture of cloth in Ire-

---

[255] In a pamphlet cited by Dr. Smith (vol. ii., p. 244, in his memoirs of wool) it is said that the total value of those manufactures exported in 1697, was £23,614 9s. 6d., namely, in friezes and stockings, £14,625 12s.; in old and new draperies, £8,988 17s. 6d.; and that though the Irish had been every year increasing, yet they had not recovered above one-third of the woollen trade which they had before the war (ib. 243). The value in 1687, according to the same authority, was £70,521 14s.; of which the friezes were £56,485 16s.; stockings, £2,520 18s.; and old and new drapery (which it is there said could alone interfere with the English trade), £11,514 10s.

[256] Preamble of English act of 1699.

land[257] both by the cheapness of all sorts of necessaries for life, and *goodness of materials for making all manner of cloth*, doth invite your subjects of England, with their families and servants, to leave their habitations to settle there, to the increase of the woollen manufacture in Ireland, which makes your loyal subjects in this kingdom very apprehensive that *the further growth* of it *may* greatly prejudice the said manufacture here; by which the trade of the nation and the value of lands will very much decrease, and the numbers of your people be much lessened here." They then beseech his majesty "in the most public and effectual way, that may be, to declare to all your subjects of Ireland, that the *growth* and *increase* of the woollen manufacture hath long, and will ever be looked upon with jealousy by all your subjects of this kingdom; *and if not timely remedied*, may occasion very strict laws, totally to prohibit and suppress the same; and, on the other hand, if they turn their industry and skill to the settling and improving the linen manufacture, for which generally the lands of that kingdom are very proper, they shall receive all countenance, favour, and protection from your *royal influence*, for the encouragement and promoting of the said linen manufacture, to *all the advantage and profit that kingdom can be capable of*."

King William in his answer says, "His Majesty will take care to do what their lordships have desired;" and the lords direct that the Lord Chancellor should order that the address and answer be forthwith printed and published.[258]

In the address of the Commons[259] they say, that "being sensible that the wealth and peace of this kingdom do, in a great measure, depend on preserving the woollen manufacture, as much as possible, *entire* to this realm, they think it becomes them, like their ancestors, to be jealous of the *establishment* and *increase* thereof elsewhere; and to use their utmost endeavours to prevent it, and therefore, they cannot without trouble observe, that Ireland, dependent on, and protected by England in the enjoyment of all they have, and which is so proper for the linen manufacture, the establishment and growth of which there would be so enriching to themselves, and so profitable to England, should *of late* apply itself to the woollen manufacture, to the great prejudice of the trade of this kingdom, and so unwillingly promote the linen trade, which would benefit both them and us.

"The consequence whereof will necessitate your parliament of England to interpose, to prevent the mischief that *threatens* us, unless your Majesty, by your authority and great wisdom, shall find means to secure the trade of England by making your subjects of Ireland to pursue the joint interest of both kingdoms.

"And we do most humbly implore your Majesty's protection and favour in this matter; and that you will make it your royal care, and enjoin all those you employ in Ireland, to make it their care, and use their utmost diligence, to hinder the *exportation of wool* from Ireland, except to be imported hither, and for the discouraging the woollen manufactures, and encouraging the linen manufactures in Ireland, to which we shall be *always* ready to give our *utmost* assistance."

This address was presented to his Majesty by the house: The answer is explicit:

[257] 9th June, 1698, vol. of Lords' Journals, p. 314.
[258] Lords' Journ., p. 315.
[259] 30th June, 1698.

"I shall do all that in me lies to discourage the woollen trade in Ireland, and encourage the linen manufacture there; and to promote the trade of England."

He soon after wrote a letter[260] to Lord Galway, then one of the lord's justices of this kingdom, in which he tells him, "that it was never of such importance to have at present a good session of parliament, not only in regard to my affairs of that kingdom, but especially of this here. The chief thing that must be tried to be prevented is, that the Irish parliament takes no notice of what has passed in this here,[261] and that you make effectual laws for the linen manufacture, and discourage *as far as possible* the woollen." It would be unjust to infer from any of those proceedings that this great prince wanted affection for this country. They were times of party. He was often under the necessity of complying against his own opinion and wishes, and about this time was obliged to send away his favourite guards, in compliance with the desire of the Commons.

The houses of parliament in England originally intended, that the business should be done in the parliament of Ireland by the exertion of that great and just influence which King William had acquired in that kingdom. On the first day of the following session[262] the lords justices, in their speech, mention a bill transmitted for the encouragement of the linen and hempen manufactures, which they recommend in the following words: "The settlement of this manufacture will contribute much to people the country, and will be found *much more advantageous to this kingdom* than the woollen manufacture, which being the settled staple trade of England, from *whence all foreign markets* are supplied, can never be encouraged *here* for that purpose; whereas the linen and hempen manufactures will not only be encouraged as consistent with the trade of England, but will render the trade of this kingdom both useful and necessary to England."

The Commons in their address[263] promise their hearty endeavours to establish a linen and hempen manufacture in Ireland, and say that they hoped to find such a temperament in respect to the woollen trade here, that the same may not be injurious to England. They referred the consideration of that subject to the committee of supply, who resolved that an additional duty be laid on old and new drapery of the manufacture of this kingdom,[264] that shall be exported, friezes excepted; to which the House agreed.[265] But there were petitions presented against this duty, and relative to the quantity of it, and the committee appointed to consider of this duty were not it seems so expeditious in their proceedings as the impatience of the times required.[266]

On the 2nd of October the lords justices made a quickening speech to both houses, taking notice, that the progress which they expected was not made, in the business of the session, and use those remarkable words: "The matters we recom-

---

[260] 16th July, 1698.
[261] Rapin's Hist., vol. xvii., p. 417.
[262] 27th September, 1698, vol. ii., p. 994.
[263] Com. Journ., vol. ii., p. 997.
[264] Ib., vol. ii., p. 1022.
[265] October 24, 1698.
[266] Com. Journ., vol. ii., pp. 1007, 1035.

mended to you are so necessary, and the prosperity of this kingdom depends so much on the good success of this session, that since we know his Majesty's affairs cannot permit your sitting very long, we thought the greatest mark we could give of our kindness and concern for you, was to come hither, and desire you to hasten the despatch of the matters under your consideration; in which we are the more earnest, because we must be sensible, that if the present opportunity his majesty's affection to you hath put into your hands be lost, it seems hardly to be recovered.[267]

On the 2nd of January, 1698, O. S. the House resolved that the report from the committee of the whole House, appointed to consider of a duty to be laid on the woollen manufactures of this kingdom, should be made on the next day, and nothing to intervene. But on that day a message was delivered from the lords justices in the following words: "We have received his majesty's commands[268] to send unto you a bill, entitled an act for laying an additional duty upon woollen manufactures exported out of this kingdom; the passing of which in this session his majesty recommended to you, as what may be of great advantage for the preservation of the trade of this kingdom."

The bill which accompanied this message was presented, and a question for receiving it was carried in the affirmative, by 74 against 34. This bill must have been transmitted from the Council of Ireland. Whilst the Commons were proceeding with the utmost temper and moderation, were exerting great firmness in restraining all attempts to inflame the minds of the people,[269] and were deliberating on the most important subject that could arise, it was taken out of their hands; but the bill passed, though not without opposition,[270] and received the royal assent on the 29th day of January, 1698.

By this act an additional duty was imposed of 4s. for every 20s. in value of broadcloth exported out of Ireland, and 2s. on every 20s. in value of new drapery, friezes only excepted, from the 25th of March, 1699, to the 25th of March, 1702;[271] the only woollen manufacture excepted was one of which Ireland had been in possession before the reign of Edward III., and in which she had been always distinguished.[272] This law has every appearance of having been framed on the part of the Administration.[273]

But it did not satisfy the English parliament, where a perpetual law was made, prohibiting, from the 20th of June, 1699,[274] the exportation from Ireland of all

[267] Com. Journ., p. 1032.
[268] Ib., vol. ii., p. 1082.
[269] Com. Journ., vol. ii., p. 1007.
[270] Ib., 1104, by 105 against 41.
[271] 10 W. 3, ch. 5.
[272] And. on Com. Journ., vol. i., 204.
[273] The Commissioners of Trade in England, by their representation of the 11th October, 1698, say (Eng. Com. Journ., vol. xii., p. 437), "they conceive it not necessary to make any alteration whatsoever in this Act," but take notice that the duties on broadcloth, of which very little is made in Ireland, is 20 per cent.; but the duty on new drapery, of which much is made, is but 10 per cent.
[274] Eng. Stat., 10 and 11 William III., ch. 10, passed in 1699.

goods made or mixed with wool, except to England and Wales, and with the licence of the Commissioners of the Revenue; duties[275] had been before aid on the importation into England equal to a prohibition, therefore this Act has operated as a total prohibition of the exportation.

Before these laws the Irish were under great disadvantages in the woollen trade, by not being allowed to export their woollen manufactures to the English colonies,[276] or to import dye stuffs directly from thence; and the English in this respect, and in having those exclusive markets, possessed considerable advantages.

Let it now be considered what are the usual means taken to promote the prosperity of any country in respect of trade and manufactures? She is encouraged to work up her own materials, to export her manufactures to other nations, to import from them the material for manufacture, and to export none of her own that she is able to work up; not to buy what she is capable of selling to others, and to promote the carrying trade and ship-building. If these are the most obvious means by which a nation may advance in strength and riches, institutions counteracting those means must necessarily tend to reduce it to weakness and poverty; and, therefore, the advocates for the continuance of those institutions will find it difficult to satisfy the world that such a system of policy is either reasonable or just.

The cheapness of labour, the excellence of materials, and the success of the manufacture in the excluded country,[277] may appear to an unprejudiced man to be rather reasons for the encouragement than for the prohibition. But the preamble of the English Act of the 10th and 11th of William III. affirms, that the exportation from Ireland and the English plantations in America to foreign markets, heretofore supplied from England, would inevitably sink the value of lands, and tend to the ruin of the trade and manufactures of that realm. I shall only consider this assertion as relative to Ireland. A fact upon which the happiness of a great and ancient kingdom, and of millions of people depends, ought to have been supported by the most incontestable evidence, and should never be suffered to rest in speculation, or to be taken from the mere suggestion or distant apprehension of commercial jealousy. Those fears for the future were not founded on any experience of the past. From what market had the woollen manufactures of Ireland ever excluded England? What part of her trade, and which of her manufactures had been ruined; and where did any of her lands fall by the woollen exports of Ireland? Were any of those facts attempted to be proved at the time of the prohibition? The amount of the Irish export proves it to have been impossible that those facts could have then existed. The consequences mentioned as likely to arise to England from the supposed increase of those manufactures in Ireland, had no other foundation but the apprehensions of rivalship among trading people, who, in excluding their fellow-citizens, have opened the gates for the admission of the enemy.

Whether those apprehensions are now well-founded, should be carefully considered. Justice, sound policy, and the general good of the British Empire require

[275] 12 Ch. II. ch. 4, Eng., and afterwards continued by 11 Geo. I., ch. 7. Brit.

[276] By an Eng. Act, made in 1663, the same which laid the first restraint on the exportation of cattle.

[277] See the Address of the English House of Lords.

it. The arguments in support of those restraints are principally these:—That labour is cheaper, and taxes lower, in Ireland than in England, and that the former would be able to undersell the latter in all foreign markets.

Spinning is now certainly cheaper in Ireland, because the persons employed in it live on food[278] with which the English would not be content; but the wages of spinners would soon rise if the trade was opened. At the loom, I am informed, that the same quantity of work is done cheaper in England than in Ireland; and we have the misfortune of daily experience to convince us that the English, notwithstanding the supposed advantages of the Irish in this trade, undersell them at their own markets in every branch of the woollen manufacture. A decisive proof that they cannot undersell the English in foreign markets.

With the increase of manufactures, agriculture, and commerce in Ireland, the demand for labour, and consequently its price, would increase.[279] That price would be soon higher in Ireland than in England. It is not in the richest countries, but in those that are growing rich the fastest, that the wages of labour are highest,[280] though the price of provisions is much lower in the latter; this, before the present rebellion, was in both respects the case of England and North America. Any difference in the price of labour is more than balanced by the difference in the price of material, which has been for many years past higher in Ireland than in England, and would become more valuable if the export of the manufacture was allowed. The English have also great advantages in this trade from their habits of diligence, superior skill, and large capital. From these circumstances, though the Scotch have full liberty to export their woollen manufactures, the English work up their wool,[281] and the Scotch make only some kind of coarse cloths for the lower classes of their people; and this is said to be for want of a capital to manufacture it at home.[282] If the woollen trade was now open to Ireland, it would be for the most part carried on by English capitals, and by merchants resident there. Nearly one-half of the stock which carried on the foreign trade of Ireland in 1672, inconsiderable as it then was, belonged to those who lived out of Ireland.[283] The greater part of the exportation and coasting trade of British America was carried on by the capitals of merchants who resided in Great Britain; even many of the stores and warehouses from which goods were retailed in some of their principal provinces, particularly in Virginia and Maryland, belonged to merchants who resided in Great Britain, and the retail trade was carried on by those who were not resident in the country.[284] It is said that in ancient Egypt, China, and Indostan, the greater part of their exportation trade was carried on by foreigners.[285] The same thing happened formerly in Ireland, where the whole commerce of the country was car-

[278] Potatoes and milk, or more frequently water.

[279] Dr. Smith's "Wealth of Nations," vol. i., p. 94.

[280] Ib., pp. 85, 86.

[281] Dr. Smith's "Wealth of Nations," vol. i., p. 445; Dr. Campbell's "Polit. Survey of Great Britain," vol. ii., p. 159; Anderson on "Industry."

[282] Smith, ib.

[283] Sir W. Petty's "Political Survey of Ireland," p. 90.

[284] Smith's "Wealth of Nations," vol. i., p. 446.

[285] Ib.

ried on by the Dutch;[286] and at present, in the victualling trade of Ireland, the Irish are but factors to the English. This is not without example in Great Britain, where there are many little manufacturing towns, the inhabitants of which have not capitals sufficient to transport the produce of their own industry to those distant markets where there is demand and consumption for it, and their merchants are properly only the agents of wealthier merchants, who reside in some of the great commercial cities.[287] The Irish are deficient in all kinds of stock, they have not sufficient for the cultivation of their lands, and are deficient in the stocks of master manufacturers, wholesale merchants, and even of retailers.

Of what Ireland gains, it is computed that one-third centres in Great Britain.[288] Of our woollen manufacture the greatest part of the profit would go directly there. But the manufacturers of Ireland would be employed, would be enabled to buy from the farmers the superfluous produce of their labour, the people would become industrious, their numbers would greatly increase, the British State would be strengthened, though probably, this country would not for many years find any great influx of wealth; it would be, however, more equally distributed, from which the people and the Government would derive many important advantages.

Whatever wealth might be gained by Ireland would be, in every respect, an accession to Great Britain. Not only a considerable part of it would flow to the seat of government, and of final judicature, and to the centre of commerce; but when Ireland should be able she would be found willing, as in justice she ought to be, to bear her part of those expenses which Great Britain may hereafter incur, in her efforts for the protection of the whole British empire. If Ireland cheerfully and spontaneously, but when she was ill able, contributed, particularly in the years 1759, 1761, 1769, and continued to do so in the midst of distress and poverty, without murmur, to the end of the year 1778, when Great Britain thought proper to relieve her from a burden which she was no longer able to bear, no doubt can be entertained of her contributing, in a much greater proportion, when the means of acquiring shall be open to her.

I form this opinion, not only from the proofs which the experience of many years, and in many signal instances has given, but the nature of the Irish Constitution, which requires that the laws of Ireland should be certified under the Great Seal of England, and the superintending protection of Great Britain, necessary to the existence of Ireland, would make it her interest to cultivate, at all times, a good understanding with her sister kingdom.

The lowness of taxes in Ireland seems to fall within the objection arising from the cheapness of labour. But the disproportion between the taxes of the two kingdoms is much overrated in Great Britain. Hearth-money in Ireland amounts to about £59,000 yearly, the sums raised by Grand Juries are said to exceed the annual sum of £140,000, and the duties on beef, butter, pork, and tallow exported, at a medium from 1772 to 1778, amount to £26,577 11s. yearly. These are payable out

---

[286] Lord Strafford's Letters, vol. i., p. 33.

[287] Smith's "Wealth of Nations," vol. i., p. 445.

[288] Sir M. Decker's "Decline of Foreign Trade," p. 155, and Anderson on "Commerce," vol. ii., p. 149.

of lands, or their immediate produce, and may well be considered as a land-tax. These, with the many other taxes payable in Ireland, compared either with the annual amount of the sums which the inhabitants can earn or expend, with the rental of the lands, the amount of the circulating specie, of personal property, or of the trade of Ireland, it is apprehended would appear not to be inferior in proportion to the taxes of England compared with any of those objects in that country.[289] The sums remitted to absentees[290] are worse than so much paid in taxes, because a large proportion of these is usually expended in the country. If this reasoning is admitted, it will require no calculation to show that Ireland pays more taxes in proportion to its small income than England does in proportion to its great one.

Of excisable commodities, the consumption by each manufacturer is not so considerable as to make the great difference commonly imagined in the price of labour. It is an acknowledged fact that Ireland pays in excises as much as she is able to bear, and that her inability to bear more arises from those very restraints. But supposing the disproportion to be as great as is erroneously imagined in Great Britain, it will not conclude in favour of the prohibition. The land-tax is nearly four times as high in some counties of England as in others, and provisions are much cheaper in some parts of that kingdom than in others, and yet they have all sufficient employment, and go to market upon equal terms. But a monopoly and not an equal market was plainly the object in 1698; it was not to prevent the Irish from underselling at foreign markets, but to prevent their selling there at all. The consequences to the excluded country have been mentioned. England has also been a great sufferer by this mistaken policy.

Mr. Dobbs, who wrote in 1729,[291] affirms that by this law of 1699, our woollen manufacturers were forced away into France, Germany, and Spain; that they had in many branches so much improved the woollen manufacture of France, as not only to supply themselves, but to vie with the English in foreign markets, and that by their correspondence, they had laid the foundation for the running of wool thither both from England and Ireland. He says that those nations were then so improved, as in a great measure to supply themselves with many sorts they formerly had from England, and since that time have deprived Britain of millions, instead of thousands that Ireland might have made.

It is now acknowledged that the French undersell the English; and as far as they are supplied with Irish wool, the loss to the British empire is double what it would be, if the Irish exported their goods manufactured. This is mentioned by Sir Matthew Decker[292] as the cause of the decline of the English, and the increase of the French woollen manufactures; and he asserts that the Irish can recover that trade out of their hands. England, since the passing of this law, has got much less

---

[289] Compare the circumstances of the two countries in one of those articles which affects all the rest. The sums raised in Great Britain in time of peace are said to amount to ten millions, in Ireland to more than one million yearly. The circulating cash of the former is estimated at twenty-three millions, of the latter at two.

[290] See post 81.

[291] Essay on the "Trade of Ireland," pp. 6, 7.

[292] "Decline of Foreign Trades," pp. 55, 56, 155.

of our wool than before.[293] In 1698, the export of our wool to England amounted to 377,520¾ stone; at a medium of eight years, to Lady-day, 1728, it was only 227,049 stone, which is 148,000 stone less than in 1698, and was a loss of more than half a million yearly to England. In the last ten years the quantity exported has been so greatly reduced, that in one of these years[294] it amounted only to 1007 st. 11 lb., and in the last year did not exceed 1665 st. 12 lb.[295] The price of wool under an absolute prohibition, is £50 or £60 per cent. under the market price of Europe, which will always defeat the prohibition.[296]

The impracticability of preventing the pernicious practice of running wool is now well understood. Of the thirty-two counties in Ireland nineteen are maritime, and the rest are washed by a number of fine rivers that empty themselves into the sea. Can such an extent of ocean, such a range of coasts, such a multitude of harbours, bays, and creeks, be effectually guarded?

The prohibition of the export of live cattle forced the Irish into the re-establishment of their woollen manufacture; and the restraint of the woollen manufacture was a strong temptation to the running of wool. The severest penalties were enacted, the British legislature, the Government, and House of Commons in Ireland, exerted all possible efforts to remove this growing evil, but in vain, until the law was made in Great Britain[297] in 1739 to take off the duties from woollen or bay yarn exported from Ireland, excepting worsted yarn of two or more threads, which has certainly given a considerable check to the running of wool, and has shown that the policy of opening is far more efficacious than that of restraining. The world is become a great commercial society; exclude trade from one channel, and it seldom fails to find another.

To show the absolute necessity of Great Britain's opening to Ireland some new means of acquiring, let the annual balance of exports and imports returned from the entries in the different custom houses, in favour of Ireland, on all her trade with the whole world, in every year from 1768 to 1778, be compared with the remittances made from Ireland to England in each of those years, it will evidently appear that those remittances could not be made out of that balance. The entries of exports made at custom houses are well known to exceed the real amount of those exports in all countries, and this excess is greater in times of diffidence, when merchants wish to acquire credit by giving themselves the appearance of being great traders.

This balance in favour of Ireland on her general trade, appears by those returns to have been, in 1776, £606,190 11s. 0¼d.; in 1777, £24,203 3s. 10¼d.; in 1778, £386,384 3s. 7d.; and, taken at a medium of eleven years, from 1768 to 1778, both in-

---

[293] Dobb's, p. 76.

[294] In 1774.

[295] Nor was this deficiency made up by the exportation of yarn. The quantities of these several articles exported from 1764 to 1778 are mentioned in the Appendix, number.

[296] Smith's "Memoirs of Wool," vol. ii., p. 554. The only way to prevent it, is to enable us to work it up at home. Ib., p. 293.

[297] This was done for the benefit of the woollen manufacture in England. Eng. Com. Journ., vol. xxii., p. 442.

clusive, it amounts to the sum of £605,083 7s. 5d. The sums remitted from Ireland to Great Britain for rents, interest of money, pensions, salaries, and profits of offices, amounted, at the lowest computation, from 1768 to 1773, to £1,100,000 yearly;[298] and from 1773, when the tontines were introduced, from which period large sums were borrowed from England, those remittances were considerably increased, and are now not less than between 12 and £13,000 yearly. Ireland then pays to Great Britain double the sum that she collects from the whole world in all the trade which Great Britain allows her. It will be difficult to find a similar instance in the history of mankind.

Those great and constant issues of her wealth without any return, not felt by any other country in such a degree, are reasons for granting advantages to Ireland to supply this consuming waste, instead of depriving her of any which Nature has bestowed.

If any of the resources which have hitherto enabled her to hear this prodigious drain are injurious to the manufactures both of England and Ireland, and highly advantageous to the rivals and enemies of both, is it wise in Great Britain by persevering in an inpracticable system of commercial policy, repugnant to the natural course and order of things, to suffer so very considerable a part of the empire to remain in such a situation?

The experiment of an equal and reasonable system of commerce is worth making; that which has been found the best conductor in philosophy is the surest guide in commerce.

Would you consult persons employed in the trade? They have in one respect an interest opposite to that of the public. To narrow the competition is advantageous to the dealers,[299] but prejudicial to the public. If Edward I. had not preferred the general welfare of his subjects to the interested opinions and petitions of the traders, all merchant traders (who were then mostly strangers) would have been sent away from London,[300] for which purpose the Commons offered him the fiftieth part of their movables.[301]

What was the information given by the trading towns in 1697 and 1698 on the subject of the woollen manufacture of Ireland? Several of their[302] petitions state that the woollen manufacture was *set-up* in Ireland, as if it had been lately introduced there; and one of them goes so far as to represent the particular time and manner of introducing it. "Many of the poor of that kingdom," says this extraordinary petition, "during the late rebellion there, fled into the west of England, where they were put to work in the woollen manufacture to learn that trade; and since

---

[298] This is stated considerably under the computation made in the list of absentees published in Dublin in 1769, which makes the amount at that time £1,208,982 14s. 6d.

[299] Smith's "Wealth of Nations," vol. i., p. 316.

[300] Anderson on Com., vol. i., p. 131.

[301] The wish of traders for a monopoly is not confined to England; in the same kingdom some parts are restrained in favour of others, as in Sweden to this hour. Abbé Resnal, vol. ii., p. 28.

[302] Eng. Com. Journ., vol. xii., pp. 64, 68.

the reduction of Ireland *endeavours were used to set up* those manufactures there.[303]

Would any man suppose that this could relate to a manufacture in which this kingdom excelled before the time of Edward III., which had been the subject of so many laws in both kingdoms, and which was always cultivated here, and before this rebellion with more success than after it? The trading towns gave accounts totally inconsistent of the state of this manufacture at that time in England: from Exeter it is represented as greatly decayed and discouraged[304] in those parts, and diminished in England. But a petition from Leeds represents this manufacture as having very much increased[305] since the revolution in all its several branches, to the general interest of England; and yet, in two days after the clothiers from three towns in Gloucestershire assert that the trade has decayed, and that the poor are almost starved.[306] The Commissioners of Trade differ in opinion from them and by their report it appears that the woollen manufacture was then very much increased and improved.[307] The traders have sometimes mistaken their own interests on those subjects. In 1698 a petition for prohibiting the importation from Ireland of all worsted and woollen yarn, represents that the poor of England are ready to perish by this importation;[308] and in 1739 several petitions were preferred against taking off the duties[309] from worsted and bay yarn exported from Ireland to England. But this has been done in the manner before mentioned, and is now acknowledged to be highly useful to England. Trading people have ever aimed at exclusive privileges. Of this there are two extraordinary instances: in the year 1698 two petitions were preferred from Folkstone and Aldborough, stating a singular grievance that they suffered from Ireland, "by the Irish catching herrings *at Waterford and Wexford,*[310] and sending them to the Streights, and thereby *forestalling* and ruining petitioners' markets;" but these petitioners had the *hard lot* of having motions in their favour rejected.

I wish that the fullest information may be had in this important investigation, but between the inconsistent accounts and opinions that will probably be given, experience only can decide; and experience will demonstrate that the removal of those restraints will promote the prosperity of both kingdoms.

I have the honour to be, my Lord, &c.

---

[303] Ib., p. 64.

[304] Ib., p. 7.

[305] Eng. Com. Journ., vol. xii., p. 527.

[306] Ib., p. 530.

[307] Ib., p. 434.

[308] Ib., p. 387.

[309] Ib., vol. xxii.

[310] Eng. Com. Journ., vol. xxii., p. 178.

SIXTH LETTER.

Dublin, 1st September, 1779.

My Lord,

By the proceedings in the English Parliament, in the year 1698, and the speech of the Lords Justices to the Irish Parliament in that year, it appears that the linen was intended to be given to this country as an equivalent for the woollen manufacture. The opinion that this supposed equivalent was accepted as such by Ireland is mistaken. The temperament which the Commons of Ireland in their address said they hoped to find was no more than a partial and temporary duty on exportation, as an experiment only, and not as an established system, reserving the exportation of frieze, then much the most valuable part to Ireland.[311] The English intended the linen manufacture as a compensation, and declared that they thought it would be much more advantageous to Ireland[312] than the woollen trade.

This idea of an equivalent has led several persons, and, among the rest, two very able writers[313] into mistakes from the want of information in some facts which are necessary to be known, that this transaction may be fully understood, and, therefore, ought to be particularly stated.

The Irish had before this period applied themselves to the linen trade. This appears by two of their statutes, in the reign of Elizabeth, one laying a duty on the export of flax and linen yarn,[314] and the other making it felony to ship them without paying such duty.[315] In the reign of Charles I. great pains were taken by Lord Strafford to encourage this manufacture, and in the succeeding reign[316] the great and munificent efforts of the first duke of Ormond were crowned with merited success. The blasts of civil dissensions nipped those opening buds of industry; and, when the season was more favourable, it is probable that, like England, they found the woollen manufacture a more useful object of national pursuit, which may be collected from the address of the English House of Commons, "that they

---

[311] The Lords Commissioners of Trade in England, by their report of the 31st August, 1697 (Eng. Com. Journ., vol., xii., p. 428), relating to the trade between England and Ireland, though they recommend the restraining of the exportation of all sorts of woollen manufactures out of Ireland, make the following exception, "except only that of their frieze, as is wont, to England."

[312] See before speech of Lords Justices.

[313] Mr. Dobbs, and after him Dr. Smith.

[314] 11 Elizabeth, session 3, ch. 10.

[315] 13 Elizabeth, session 5, ch. 4.

[316] 17 and 18, ch. 2; ch. 9 for the advancement of the linen manufacture. Carte.

so unwillingly promote the linen trade,"[317] and it was natural for a poor and exhausted country to work up the materials of which it was possessed.

In 1696 the English had given encouragement to the manufactures of hemp and flax in Ireland, but without stipulating any restraint of the export of woollen goods. The English Act made in that year recites that great sums of money were yearly exported out of England for the purchasing of hemp, flax, and linen, and the productions thereof, which might be prevented by being supplied from Ireland, and allows natives of England and Ireland to import into England, free of all duties,[318] hemp and flax, and all the productions thereof. In the same session[319] a law passed in England for the more effectually preventing the exportation of wool, and for encouraging the importation thereof from Ireland. Both those manufactures were under the consideration of Parliament this session, and it was thought, from enlarged views of the welfare of both kingdoms, that England should encourage the linen without discouraging the woollen manufacture of Ireland. There was no further encouragement given by England to our linen manufacture for some years after the year 1696.[320] *In 1696 there was no equivalent whatever given* for the prohibition of the export of our woollen manufactures.

It is true the assurances given by both Houses of Parliament in England for the encouragement of our linen trade were as strong as words could express; but was this intended encouragement, if immediately carried into execution, an equivalent to Ireland for what she had lost? Let it first be considered whether it was an equivalent at the time of the prohibition.

The woollen was then the principal manufacture and trade of Ireland. That it was then considered as her staple, appears from the several Acts of Parliament before mentioned, and from the attempt made in 1695 by the Irish House of Commons to lay a duty on all old and new drapery imported. The amount of the export proves[321] the value of the trade to so poor a country as Ireland, and makes it probable that she then clothed her own people. The address of the English House of Lords shows that this manufacture was "growing" amongst us, and the goodness of our own materials "for making *all manner* of cloth."[322] And the English Act of 1698 is a voucher that this manufacture was then in so flourishing a state as to give apprehensions, however ill founded, of its rivalling England in foreign markets. The immediate consequences to Ireland showed the value of what she lost; many thousands of manufacturers were obliged to leave this kingdom for want of employment; many parts of the southern and western counties were so far depopulated that they have not yet recovered a reasonable number of inhabitants; and the whole kingdom was reduced to the greatest poverty and distress.[323] The linen trade of Ireland was then of little consideration, compared with the woollen.[324]

---

[317] See before.

[318] 7 and 8 W. 3, ch. 39, from the 1st of August, 1696.

[319] 7 and 8 W., ch. 28.

[320] Not till the year 1705.

[321] Com. Journ., vol. ii., p. 725, 733; vol. xvi., p. 360.

[322] See before.

[323] Dobbs, 6, 7.

[324] Com. Journ., vol. xvi., p. 362.

The whole exportation of linens, in 1700,[325] amounted only in value to £14,112. It was an experiment substituted in the place of an established trade.

The English ports in Asia, Africa, and America were then shut against our linens; and, when they were opened[326] for our white and brown linens, the restraints of imports from thence to Ireland made that concession of less value, and she still found it her interest to send, for the most part, her linens to England. The linen could not have been a compensation for the woollen manufacture, which employs by far a greater number of hands, and yields much greater profit to the public, as well as to the manufacturers.[327] Of this manufacture there are not many countries which have the primum in equal perfection with England and Ireland; and no countries, taking in the various kinds of those extensive manufactures, so fit for carrying them on. There cannot be many rivals in this trade: in the linen they are most numerous. Other parts of the world are more fit for it than Ireland, and many equally so.

If this could be supposed to have been an equivalent at the time, or to have become so by its success, it can no longer be considered in that light. The commercial state of Europe is greatly altered. Ireland can no longer enjoy the benefit intended for her. It was intended that the great sums of money remitted out of England to foreign countries in this branch of commerce should all centre in Ireland, and that England should be supplied with linen from thence;[328] but foreigners now draw great sums from England in this trade, and rival the Irish in the English markets. The Russians are becoming powerful rivals to the Irish, and undersell them in the coarse kinds of linen. This is now the staple manufacture of Scotland. England, that had formerly cultivated this manufacture without success, and had taken linens[329] from France to the amount of £700,000 yearly, has now made great progress in it. The encouragement of this trade in England and Scotland has been long a principal object to the British Legislature; and the nation that encouraged us to the undertaking has now become our rival in it.[330] That this is not too strong an expression will appear by considering two British statutes, one of which[331] has laid a duty on the importation of Irish sail-cloth into Great Britain, as long as the bounties should be paid on the exportation from[332] Ireland, which obliged us to discontinue them; and the other[333] has given a bounty on the exportation of *British* chequered and striped linens exported out of *Great Britain* to Africa, America,

[325] Ib., p. 363.
[326] By 3rd and 4th Anne, ch. 9.
[327] And. on Comm., vol. ii., p. 225.
[328] This appears by the preamble to the English Act of the 7th and 8th W. 3, ch. 39.
[329] Anderson on Commerce, vol. ii., p. 177.
[330] Com. Journ., vol. xvi., p. 365.
[331] In 1750.
[332] By the law of 1750, and the bounties given on the exportation of sail-cloth from Great Britain to foreign countries, Ireland has almost lost this trade; she cannot now supply herself. Great Britain has not been the gainer; the quantities of sail-cloth imported there, in 1774, exceeding, according to the return from the Custom House in London, the quantities imported in the year 1750, when the restrictive law was made. It has been taken from Ireland and given to the Russians, Germans, and Dutch (Ir. Com. Journ., vol. xvi., p. 363).
[333] 10 G. 3, ch. — continued by act of last session to the year 1786.

Spain, Portugal, Gibraltar, the island of Minorca, or the East Indies. This is now become a very valuable part of the manufacture, which Great Britain, by the operation of this bounty, keeps to herself. The bounties on the exportation of all other linen, which she has generously given to ours as well as to her own,[334] operate much more strongly in favour of the latter;[335] the expense of freight, insurance, commission, &c., in sending the linens from Ireland to England has been computed at four per cent.; and if this computation is right, when the British linens obtain £12 per cent., the full amount of the premium, the Irish do not receive above eight. Those bounties, though acknowledged to be a favour to Ireland, give Great Britain a further and a very important advantage in this trade, by inducing us to send all our linens to England, from whence other countries are supplied.

The great hinge upon which the stipulation on the part of England, in the year 1698, turned was, that England should give every possible encouragement to the linen and hempen manufactures in Ireland. Encouraging those manufactures in another country was not compatible with this intention. The course of events made it necessary to do this in Scotland;[336] the course of trade made it necessary for England to do the same. A commercial country must cultivate every considerable manufacture of which she has or can get the primum. These circumstances have totally changed the state of the question; and if it was reasonable and just that Ireland, in 1698, should have accepted of the linen in the place of the woollen manufactures, it deserves to be considered whether by the almost total change of the circumstances it is not now unreasonable and unjust.

America itself, the opening of whose markets[337] to Irish linens was thought to have been one of the principal encouragements to that trade, is now become a rival and an enemy; and when she puts off the latter character, will appear in the former with new force and infinite advantages.

The emigration for many years of such great multitudes of our linen manufacturers to America,[338] proves incontrovertibly that they can carry on their trade with more success in America than in Ireland. But let us examine the facts to determine whether the proposed encouragements have taken place. The declaration of the Lords of England for the encouragement of the linen manufacture of Ireland was "to all the advantage and profit that kingdom can be capable of;" and of the Commons, "that they shall be *always* ready to give it their *utmost* assistance." The speech of the Lords Justices shows the extent of this engagement, and promises the encouragement of England "to the linen and hempen manufactures of Ireland."

In the year 1705[339] liberty was given to the natives of England or Ireland to export from Ireland to the English plantations white and brown linens only, but

---

[334] In the year 1743.

[335] Com. Journ., vol. xvi., 369, pp. 389.

[336] *To please the English* Scotland has for half a century past exerted herself as much as possible to improve the linen manufacture.—Anderson on Industry, vol. ii., p. 233.

[337] Com. Journ., vol. xvi., p. 370.

[338] The province of Ulster, in two years, is said to have lost 30,000 of its inhabitants. Com. Journ., vol. xvi., p. 381.

[339] From 24th June, 1705, 3 and 4 Anne, ch. 8, for 11 years, but afterwards continued.

no liberty given to bring in return any goods from thence to Ireland, which will appear from the account in the Appendix to have made this law of inconsiderable effect. In 1743 premiums were given on the exportation of English and Irish linens from Great Britain; and the bounty granted by Great Britain, in 1774, on flax seed imported into Ireland is a further proof of the munificent attention of Great Britain to our linen trade. But chequered, striped, printed, painted, stained, or dyed linens were not until lately admitted into the plantations from Ireland; and the statutes of Queen Anne,[340] laying duties at the rate of thirty per cent. on such linens made in *foreign* parts and imported into Great Britain, have been, rather by a forced construction, extended to Ireland, which is deprived of the British markets[341] for those goods, and, until the year 1777,[342] was excluded from the American markets also. But it is thought, as to chequered and striped linens, which are a valuable branch of the linen trade, that this Act will have little effect in favour of this country, from the operation of the before-mentioned British Act of the 10th G. 3, which, by granting a bounty on the exportation of those goods of the manufacture of Great Britain only gives a direct preference to the British linen manufacture before the Irish.

The hempen manufacture of Ireland has been, so far, *discouraged* by Great Britain, that the Irish have totally abandoned the culture of hemp.[343]

I hope to be excused for weighing scrupulously a proposed equivalent, for which the receiver was obliged to part with the advantages of which he was possessed. The equivalent, given in 1667, for the almost entire exclusion of Ireland from the ports of England and America, was the exportation of our manufactures to foreign nations. The prohibition of 1699 was not altogether consistent with the equivalent of 1667; and from the equivalent of 1698 the superior encouragement since given to English and Scotch linen, and the discouragement to the chequer and stamped linen and sail-cloth of Ireland must make a large deduction. But why must one manufacture only be encouraged? The linen and the woollen trades of Ireland were formerly both encouraged by the legislatures of both kingdoms; they are now both equally encouraged in England.

If this single trade was found sufficient employment for 1,000,000 men who remained in this country at the time of this restraint (the contrary of which has been shown), it would require the interposition of more than human wisdom to divide it among 2,500,000 men at this day, and to send the multitude away satisfied.

No populous commercial country can subsist on one manufacture; if the world has ever produced such an instance I have not been able to find it. Reason and experience demonstrate that, to make society happy, the members of it must be able to supply the wants of each other, as far as their country affords the means; and, where it does not, by exchanging the produce of their industry for that of their neighbours. When the former is discouraged, or the latter prevented, that community cannot be happy. If they are not allowed to send to other countries the manufactured produce of their own, the people who enjoy that liberty will under-

[340] Brit. Acts, 10 Anne, ch. 19; 11 and 12 Anne, ch. 9; 6 G. 1, ch. 4.
[341] Brit. Act. 18 G. 3, ch. 53.
[342] Ir. Com. Journ., vol xvi., pp. 363, 364.
[343] Ib., p. 365.

sell them in their own markets; the restrained manufacturers will be reduced to poverty, and will hang like paralytic limbs on the rest of the body.

If England's commercial system would have been incomplete, had she failed to cultivate any one principal manufacture of which she had or could obtain the material, what shall we say to the commercial state of that country, restrained in a manufacture of which she has the materials in abundance, and in which she had made great progress, and almost confined to one manufacture of which she has not the primum.

Manufactures, though they may flourish for a time, generally fail in countries that do not produce the principal materials of them. Of this there are many instances. Venice and the other Italian states carried on the woollen manufacture until the countries which produced the materials manufactured them, when the Italian manufactures declined, and dwindled into little consideration in comparison of their former splendour. The Flemings, from their vicinity to those countries that produced the materials, beat the Italians out of their markets. But when England cultivated that manufacture, the Flemings lost it. That this, and not oppression, was the cause, appears from the following state of the linen manufacture[344] there, because it consumes flax, the native produce of the soil; and it is much to be feared that those islands will be obliged to yield the superiority in this trade to other nations that have great extent of country, and sufficient land to spare for this impoverishing production.

That some parts of Ireland may produce good flax must be allowed, and also that parts of Flanders would produce fine wool. But though the legislature has for many years made it a capital object to encourage the growth of flax and the raising of flax-seed in this kingdom, yet it is obliged to pay above £9,000 yearly in premiums on the importation of flax-seed, which is now almost imported, and costs us between £70,000 and £80,000 yearly. Flax farming, in any large quantity, is become a precarious and losing trade,[345] and those who have been induced to attempt it by premiums from the Linen Board have, after receiving those premiums, generally found themselves losers, and have declined that branch of tillage.

When the imported flax-seed is unsound and fails, in particular districts, which very frequently happens, the distress, confusion, and litigation that arise among manufacturers, farmers, retailers, and merchants, affords a melancholy proof of the dangerous consequences to a populous nation when the industry of the people and the hope of the rising year rest on a single manufacture, for the materials of which we must depend upon the courtesy and good faith of other nations.

Let me appeal to the experience of very near a century in the very instance now before you. A single manufacture is highly encouraged; it obtains large premiums, not only from the legislature of its own country, but from that of a great neighbouring kingdom; it becomes not only the first, but almost the sole national object; immense sums of money are expended in the cultivation of it,[346] and

[344] Anderson on Industry, vol. i., pp. 34 to 40.

[345] Com. Journ., vol. xvi., p. 370.

[346] See Com. Journ., vol. xvii., pp. 263 to 287, for the sums paid from 1700 to 1775. They amount to £803,486 0s. 2¾d.

the success exceeds our most sanguine expectations. But look into the state of this country; you will find property circulating slowly and languidly, and in the most numerous classes of your people no circulation or property at all. You will frequently find them in want of employment and of food, and reduced in a vast number of instances from the slightest causes to distress and beggary. All other manufacturers will continue spiritless, poor, and distressed, and derive from uncertain employment a precarious and miserable subsistence; they gain little by the success of the prosperous trade, the dealers in which are tempted to buy from that country to which they principally sell; the disease of those morbid parts must spread through the whole body, and will at length reach the persons employed in the favoured manufacture. These will become poor and wretched, and discontented; they emigrate by thousands; in vain you represent the crime of deserting their country, the folly of forsaking their friends, the temerity of wandering to distant, and, perhaps, inhospitable climates; their despondency is deaf to the suggestions of prudence, and will answer, that they can no longer stay "where hope never comes," but will fly from these "regions of sorrow."[347]

Let me not be thought to undervalue the bounties and generosity of that great nation which has taken our linen trade under its protection. There is much ill-breeding, though, perhaps, some good sense, in the churlish reply of the philosopher to the request of the prince who visited his humble dwelling, and desired to know, and to gratify his wishes; that they were no more than this, that the prince should not stand between the philosopher and the sun. Had he been a man of the world he might have expressed the same idea with more address, though with less force and significance; he might have said, "I am sensible of your greatness and of your power; I have no doubts of your liberality; but Nature has abundantly given me all that I wish; intercept not one of her greatest gifts; allow me to enjoy the bounties of her hand, and the contentment of my own mind will furnish the rest."

I have the honour to be, my Lord, &c.

---

[347] This malady of emigration among our linen manufacturers has appeared at many different periods during this century.

SEVENTH LETTER.

Dublin, 3rd September, 1779.

My Lord,

By comparing the restrictive law of 1699 with the statutes which had been previously enacted in England from the fifteenth year of the reign of Charles II., relative to the colonies, it appears that this restrictive law originated in a system of colonisation. The principle of that system was that the colonies should send their materials to England and take from thence her manufactures, and that the making those manufactures in the colonies should be prohibited or discouraged. But was it reasonable to extend this principle to Ireland? The climate, growth, and productions of the colonies were different from those of the parent country. England had no sugar-canes, coffee, dying stuff, and little tobacco. She took all those from her colonies only, and it was thought reasonable that they should take from her only the manufactures which she made. But in Ireland the climate, soil, growth, and productions are the same as in England, who could give no such equivalent to Ireland as she gave to America, and was so far from considering her when this system first prevailed, as a proper subject for such regulations, that she was allowed the benefits arising from those colonies equally with England, until the fifteenth year of the reign of King Charles II.[348] By an Act passed in that year, Ireland had no longer the privilege of sending any of her exports, except servants, horses, victuals, and salt, to any of the colonies; the reasons are assigned in the preamble "to make this kingdom a staple, not only of the commodities of those plantations, but also of the commodities of other countries and places for the supplying of them, and it being the usage of other nations to keep their plantation trade to themselves."[349] At the time of passing this law, though less liberal ideas in respect of Ireland were then entertained, it went no further than not to extend to her the benefits of those colony regulations; but it was not then thought that this kingdom was a proper subject for any such regulations. The scheme of substituting there, instead of the woollen, the linen trade, was not at that time thought of. The English were desirous to establish it among themselves, and by an Act of Parliament,[350] made in that year for encouraging the manufacture of linen, granted to all foreigners who shall set up in England the privileges of natural born subjects.

But it appears by the English Statute of the 7th and 8th of William III.,[351] which

---

[348] 12 Ch. II., ch. 7.

[349] As other nations did the same, Ireland was shut out from the New World and a considerable part of the Old in Asia and Africa.

[350] 15 Ch. II., ch. 15.

[351] Ch. 39.

has been before stated, that this scheme had not succeeded in England, and from this act it is manifest that England considered itself as well as Ireland interested to encourage the linen manufacture there; and it does not then appear to have been thought just that Ireland should purchase this benefit for both, by giving up the exportation of any other manufacture. But in 1698 a different principle prevailed, in effect the same, so far as relates to the woollen manufacture, with that which had prevailed as to the commerce of the colonies. This is evident from the preamble of the English law,[352] made in 1699, "for as much as wool and woollen manufactures of cloth, serge, bays, kersies, and other stuffs, made or mixed with wool, are the greatest and most profitable commodities of this kingdom, on which the value of lands and the trade of the nation do chiefly depend, and whereas great quantities of like manufactures have of late been made and are daily increasing in the kingdom of Ireland, and *in the English plantations* in America, and are exported from thence to foreign markets heretofore supplied from England, which will inevitably sink the value of lands, and tend to the ruin of the trade and woollen manufactures of this realm; for the prevention whereof and for the encouragement of the woollen manufactures in this kingdom, &c.

The ruinous consequences of the woollen manufactures of Ireland to the value of lands, trade, and manufactures of England, stated in this Act, are apprehensions that were entertained, and not events that had happened; and before those facts are taken for granted, I request the mischief recited in the Acts[353] made in England to prevent the importation of cattle dead or alive from Ireland, may be considered. The mischiefs stated in those several laws are supposed to be as ruinous to England as those recited in the Act of 1699, and yet are now allowed to be groundless apprehensions occasioned by short and mistaken views of the real interests of England. Sir W. Petty[354] demonstrates that the opinion entertained in England at the time of his prohibition of the import of cattle from Ireland was ill-founded; he calls it a strange conceit. If he was now living, he would probably consider the prohibition of our woollen exports as not having a much better foundation.

Connecting this preamble of the Act of 1699, with the speech made from the throne to the parliament of Ireland in the year 1698, with the addresses of both houses in England, and with the prohibition by this and by other Acts, formerly made in England, of exporting wool from Ireland except to that kingdom, the object of this new commercial regulation is obvious. It was to discourage the woollen manufacture in Ireland and in effect to prohibit the exportation from thence because it was the principal branch of manufacture and trade in England; to induce us to send to them our materials for that manufacture, and that we should be supplied with it by them; and to encourage, as a compensation to Ireland, the linen manufacture, which was not at that time a commercial object of any importance

[352] 10th and 11th Wm. III., ch. 10.

[353] 15 Ch. II., ch. 7. 18 Ch. II., ch. 2. 20 Ch. II., ch. 7. 22nd & 23rd Ch. II., ch. 2.

[354] Petty's "Political Survey of Ireland," p. 70, and *ib*. "Report from the Council of Trade," pages 117, 118. Sir W. Temple, vol. iii, pp. 22, 23, that England was evidently a loser by the prohibition of cattle.

Dr. Smith's "Memoirs of Wool," vol. ii, p. 337, that the English have since sufficiently felt the mischiefs of this proceeding.

to England. This I take to be a part of the system of colony regulations. Whether it was reasonable or just to bring this kingdom into that system, has been already submitted from arguments drawn from the climates and productions of the different countries. The supposed compensation was no more than what Ireland had before; no further encouragement was given by England to our linen manufacture until six years after this prohibition, when at the request of the Irish House of Commons and after a representation of the ruinous state of the country, liberty was given by an English Act of Parliament[355] to export our white and brown linens into the colonies, which was allowing us to do as to one manufacture what, before the fifteenth of King Charles II., was permitted in every instance.

It would be presumption in a private man to decide on the weight of those arguments; but to select and arrange facts that lie dispersed in journals and books of Statutes in both kingdoms, and to make observations on those facts with caution and respect, can never give offence to those who inquire for the purpose of relieving a distressed nation and of promoting the general welfare. In that confidence I beg leave to place this subject in a different view, and to request that it may be considered what the commercial system of this kingdom was at the time of passing this law of 1699, and whether it was, in this respect, reasonable or just that such a regulation should have been then made? The great object which the Lords and Commons of Great Britain have determined to investigate led to such a discussion; determined as they are to pursue effectual methods "for promoting the common strength, wealth, and commerce of both kingdoms." What better guides can they follow than the examples of their ancestors and the means used by them for many centuries, and in the happiest times, for attaining the same great purposes.

In my opinion it would be improper, in the present state of the British Empire, to agitate disputed questions that may inflame the passions of men. May no such questions ever arise between two affectionate sister kingdoms. It is my purpose only to state acknowledged facts, which never have been contested, and from those facts to lay before you the commercial system of Ireland before the year 1699.

For several centuries before this period Ireland was in possession of the English Common law[356] and of Magna Charta. The former secures the subject in the enjoyment of property of every kind; and by the latter *the liberties of all the ports of the kingdom are established.*

The Statutes made in England for the common and public weal are,[357] by an Irish Act of the 10th of Henry VII., made laws in Ireland; and the English Commercial Statutes, in which Ireland is expressly mentioned, will place the former state of commerce in this country in a light very different from that in which it has been generally considered in Great Britain.

By the 17th of Edward III., ch. 1, all sorts of merchandises may be exported from Ireland, except to the King's enemies.

---

[355] 3 and 4 Anne, ch. 8.

[356] 4 Inst., 349. Matth. Paris, anno. 1172, pp. 121, 220. Vit. H. 2. Pryn, against the 4 Inst., c. 76, pp. 250, 252. Sir John Davis's Hist., p. 71. Lord Lyttleton's Hist. of, H. 2. vol. iii., pp. 89, 90. 7 Co., 22, 23. 4th Black, 429.

[357] Cooke's 4th Inst., 351.

By the 27th of Edward III., ch. 18, merchants of Ireland and Wales may bring their merchandise to the staple of England; and by the 34th of the same king, ch. 17, all kinds of merchandises may be exported from and imported into Ireland, as well by aliens as denizens. In the same year there is another Statute, ch. 18, that all persons who have lands or possessions in Ireland might freely import thither and export from that kingdom *their own commodities*; and by the 50th of Edward III., ch. 8, no alnage is to be paid, if frieze ware, which are made in Ireland.

This freedom of commerce was beneficial to both countries. It enabled Ireland to be very serviceable to Edward III., as it had been to his father and grandfather, in supplying numbers of armed vessels for transporting their great lords and their attendants and troops[358] to Scotland and also to Portsmouth for his French wars.

But the reign of Edward IV. furnishes still stronger instances of the regard shown by England to the trade and manufactures of this country.

In the third year of that monarch's reign the artificers of England complained to parliament that they were greatly impoverished, and *could not live* by bringing in divers commodities and wares ready wrought.[359] An Act passed reciting those complaints, and ordaining that no merchant born a subject of the king, denisen or stranger, or other person, should bring into England or Wales any woollen cloths, &c., and enumerates many other manufactures on pain of forfeiture, provided that all wares and "chaffers" made and wrought in Ireland or Wales may be brought in and sold in the realm of England, as they were wont before the making of that Act.[360]

In the next year another Act[361] passed in that kingdom, that all woollen cloth brought into England, and set to sale, should be forfeited, except cloths made in Wales or Ireland.

In those reigns England was as careful of the commerce and manufactures of her ancient sister kingdom, particularly in her great staple trade, as she was of her own.

Of this attention there were further instances in the years 1468 and 1478. In two treaties concluded in those years between England and the Duke of Bretagne, the merchandise to be traded in between England, Ireland, and Calais on the one part, and Bretagne on the other, is specified, and woollen cloths are particularly mentioned.[362]

And in a treaty between Henry VII. and the Netherlands, Ireland is included, both as to exports and imports.[363]

The commercial Acts of Parliament in which Ireland is mentioned have only

---

[358] Anderson on Commerce, vol. i., p. 174.

[359] 3rd Edward IV., ch. 4.

[360] The part of this law which mentions that it shall be determinable, at the King's pleasure, has the prohibition for its object, and does not lessen the force of the argument in favour of Ireland.

[361] 4th Edward IV., ch. 1.

[362] Anderson on Commerce, vol. i., p. 285.

[363] Ib., p. 319.

been stated, because they are not generally known. But the laws made in England before the 10th Henry VII. for the protection of merchants and the security of trade, being laws for the common and public weal, are also made laws here by the Irish statute of that year, which was returned under the great seal of England, and must have been previously considered in the privy council of that kingdom. At this period, then, the English commercial system and the Irish, so far as it depended upon the English statute law, was the same; and before this period, so far as it depended upon the common law and Magna Charta, was also the same.

From that time until the 15th of King Charles II., which takes in a period of 167 years, the commercial constitution of Ireland was as much favoured and protected as that of England. "The free enlargement of common traffic which his Majesty's subjects of Ireland enjoyed," is taken notice of incidentally in an English statute, in the reign of King James I.,[364] and in 1627, King Charles I. made a strong declaration in favour of the trade and manufactures of this country. By several English statutes in the reign of King Charles II., an equal attention was shown to the woollen manufactures in both kingdoms; in the 12th year of his reign[365] the exportation of wool, wool-felts, fuller's earth, or any kind of scowering earth, was prohibited from both. But let the reasons mentioned in the preamble for passing this law be adverted to: "For preventing inconveniences and losses that happened, and that daily do and may happen, to the kingdom of England, dominion of Wales, and kingdom of Ireland, through the secret exportation of wool out of and from the said kingdoms and dominions; and for the *better setting on work the poor people* and inhabitants of the kingdoms and dominions aforesaid, and to the intent that the full use and benefit of *the principal native commodities* of the same kingdom and dominion may come, redound, and be unto the subjects and inhabitants of the same."

This was the voice of nature, and the dictate of sound and general policy; it proclaimed to the nations that they should not give to strangers the bread of their own children; that the produce of the soil should support the inhabitants of the country; that their industry should be exercised on their own materials, and that the poor should be employed, clothed, and fed.

The shipping and navigation of England and Ireland were at this time equally favoured and protected. By another Act of the same year no goods or commodities[366] of the growth, production or manufacture of Asia, Africa, or America, shall be imported into England, *Ireland*, or Wales, but in ships which belong to the people of England or *Ireland*, the dominion of Wales, or town of Berwick-upon-Tweed, or which are of the built of the said lands, and of which the master and three-fourths of the mariners are English; and a subsequent statute[367] makes the encouragement to navigation in both countries equal, by ordaining that the subjects of Ireland and of the Plantations shall be accounted English within the meaning of that clause. Another law[368] of the same reign shows that the navigation, com-

[364] 3rd James, ch. 6.
[365] 12th Ch. II., ch.
[366] 12th Ch. II., ch. 18.
[367] 13th and 14th Ch. II., ch. 11.
[368] Ib., ch. 18.

merce, and woollen manufactures of both kingdoms were equally protected by the English legislature. This Act lays on the same restraint as the above-mentioned Act of the 12th of Charles II., and makes the transgression still more penal. It recites that wool, wool-felts, &c., are secretly exported from England and Ireland to foreign parts to the great decay of the woollen manufactures, and the destruction of the navigation and commerce of *these kingdoms*.

From those laws it appears that the commerce, navigation, and manufactures of this country were not only favoured and protected by the English legislature, but that we had in those times the full benefit of their Plantation trade; whilst the woollen manufactures were protected and encouraged in England and Ireland, the planting of tobacco in both was prohibited, because "it was one of the main products of several of the Plantations, and upon which their welfare and subsistence do depend."[369]

This policy was liberal, just, and equal; it opened the resources and cultivated the strength of every part of the empire.

This commercial system of Ireland was enforced by several Acts of her own legislature; two statutes passed in the reign of Henry VIII. to prevent the exportation of wool, because, says the first of those laws, "it hath been the cause of dearth of cloth and idleness of many folks,"[370] and "tends to the desolation and ruin of this poor land." The second of those laws enforces the prohibition[371] by additional penalties; it recites "that the said beneficial law had taken little effect, but that since the making thereof great plenty of wool had been conveyed out of this land to the great and inestimable hurt, decay, and impoverishment of the King's poor subjects within the said land, for redress whereof, and in consideration that conveying of the wool of the growth of this land out of the same is one of the greatest occasions of the idleness of the people, waste, ruin, and desolation of the King's cities and borough towns, and other places of his dominion within this land." The 11th of Elizabeth[372] lays duties on the exportation equal to a prohibition, and the reason given in the preamble ought to be mentioned: "That the said commodities may be more abundantly wrought in this realm ere they shall be so transported than presently they are, which shall set many now living idle on work, to the great relief and commodity of this realm.[373]

By the preamble of one of those Acts,[374] made in the reign of Charles II., it appears that the sale of Irish woollen goods in foreign markets was encouraged by England, "whereas there is a general complaint in *England*, France, and other parts beyond the seas (whither the woollen cloths and other commodities made of wool in this, his Majesty's kingdom of Ireland, are transported) of the false,

---

[369] 12th Ch. II., ch. 27.

[370] Ir. Act, 13th H. VIII, ch. 2.

[371] 28th H. VIII., ch. 17.

[372] Ch. 10.

[373] The necessity of encouraging the people of Ireland to manufacture their own wool appears by divers statutes to have been the sense of the legislature of both kingdoms for some centuries.

[374] Ir. Act of 17 and 18 Ch. II., ch. 15.

deceitful, uneven, and uncertain making thereof, which cometh to pass by reason that the clothiers and makers thereof do not observe any certain assize for length, breadth, and weight for making their clothes and other commodities aforesaid in this kingdom, as they do in the realm of England, and as they ought also to do here, by which means the merchants, buyers, and users of the said cloth and other commodities are much abused and deceived, and the credit, esteem, and sale of the said cloth and commodities is thereby much impaired and undervalued, to the great and general hurt and hindrance of the trade of clothing in this whole realm."

After the ports of England were shut against our cattle, and our trade to the English colonies was restrained, still this commercial system was adhered to by encouraging the manufactures of this country, and the exportation of them to foreign countries. In 1667, when the power of the Crown was not so well understood as at present, the proclamation before mentioned was published by the Lord Lieutenant and Privy Council of Ireland,[375] in pursuance of a letter from Charles II., by the advice of his council in England, notifying to all his subjects of this kingdom the allowance of a free trade to all foreign countries, either at war or peace with his Majesty.

In the year 1663 the distinction between the trade of England and Ireland,[376] and the restraints on that of the latter commenced. By an English Act passed in that year, entitled an Act "for the encouragement of trade," a title not very applicable to the parts of it that related to Ireland; besides laying a prohibition on cattle imported into England from that kingdom, the exportation of all commodities except victuals, servants, horses, and salt for the fisheries of New England and Newfoundland, from thence to the English plantations, was prohibited from the 25th March, 1764. The exports allowed were useful to them, but prejudicial to Ireland, as they consisted of our people, our provisions, and a material for manufacture which we might have used more profitably on our own coasts.

In 1670, another Act[377] passed in England to prohibit from the 24th of March, 1671, the exportation from the English plantations to Ireland of several materials for manufactures[378] without first unloading in England or Wales. We are informed by this Act that the restraint of the exportation from the English plantations to Ireland was intended by the Act of 1663; but the intention is not effectuated, though the importation of those commodities into Ireland *from England*, without first unloading there is, in effect, prohibited by that Act.

The prohibition of importing into Ireland any plantation goods, unless the same had been first landed in England, and had paid the duties, is made general, without any exception, by the English Act of the 7th and 8th W. III., ch. 22.

But by subsequent British Acts[379] it is made lawful to import from his Majesty's plantations all goods of their growth or manufactures, the articles enumerated

---

[375] Carte, vol. ii., p. 344.

[376] 15th Ch. II., ch. 7.

[377] 22nd and 23rd Ch. II., ch. 26.

[378] Sugar, tobacco, cotton, wool, indigo, steel or Jamaica wood, fustick or other dying wood, the growth of the said plantations.

[379] 4th Geo. II., ch. 15; 6th Geo. II., ch. 15; 4th Geo. II., ch. 15.

in those several Acts excepted.[380]

By a late British Act[381] there is a considerable extension of the exports from Ireland to the British plantations. But it is apprehended that this law will not answer the kind intentions of the British legislature. Denying the import from those countries to Ireland is, in effect, preventing the export from Ireland to those countries. Money cannot be expected for our goods there, we must take theirs in exchange; and this can never answer on the terms of our being obliged, in our return, to pass by Ireland, to land those goods in England, to ship them a second time, and then to sail back again to Ireland. No trade will bear such an unnecessary delay and expense. The quickness and the security of the return are the great inducements to every trade. One is lost and the other hazarded by such embarrassments; those who are not subject to them carry on the trade with such advantages over those who are so entangled as totally to exclude them from it. This is no longer the subject of speculation, it has been proved by the experience of above seventy years. Since the year 1705, when liberty was given to import white and brown linen from Ireland into the English plantations, the quantities sent there directly from Ireland were at all times very inconsiderable notwithstanding this liberty; they were sent for the most part from Ireland to England before any bounty was given on the exportation from thence, which did not take place until the year 1743; and from England the English plantations were supplied. There cannot be a more decisive proof that the liberty of exporting without a direct import in return, will not be beneficial to Ireland.

This country is the part of the British empire most conveniently situated for trade with the colonies. If not suffered to have any beneficial intercourse with them, she will be deprived of one of the great advantages of her situation; and such an obstruction to the prosperity of so considerable a part must necessarily diminish the strength of the whole British empire.

Those laws laid Ireland under restraints highly prejudicial to her commerce and navigation. From those countries the materials for ship-building[382] and some of those used in perfecting their staple manufactures were had; Ireland was, by those laws, excluded from almost all the trade of three quarters of the globe, and from all direct beneficial intercourse with her fellow-subjects in those countries,

[380] The articles in the last note, and also rice, molasses, beaver skins, and other furs, copper ore, pitch, tar, turpentine, masts, yards, and bowsprits, pimento, cocoa-nuts, whale fins, raw silk, hides and skins, pot and pearl ashes, iron and lumber.

[381] From the 24th of June, 1778, it shall be lawful to export from Ireland directly into any of the British plantations in America or the West Indies, or into any of the settlements belonging to Great Britain on the coast of Africa, any goods being the produce or manufacture of Ireland (wool and woollen manufactures in all its branches, mixed or unmixed, cotton manufactures of all sorts, mixed or unmixed, hats, glass, hops; gunpowder, and coals only excepted); and all goods, &c., of the growth, produce, or manufacture of Great Britain which may be legally imported from thence into Ireland (woollen manufacture in all its branches and glass excepted), and all foreign certificate goods that may be legally imported from Great Britain into Ireland. Two of the principal manufactures are excepted, and one of them closely connected with, if not a part of, the linen manufacture. — 18th Geo. III., ch. 55.

[382] This appears by the English Acts (3 and 4 Anne, ch. 10, 8 Anne, ch. 1, 2 Geo. II., ch. 35), giving bounties on the importation of those articles into Great Britain.

which were partly stocked from her own loins. But still, though deprived at that time of the benefit of those colonies, she was not then considered as a colony herself, her manufacturers were not in any other manner discouraged, her ports were left open, and she was at liberty to look for a market among strangers, though not among her fellow-subjects in Asia, Africa, or America.[383] By the law of 1699 she was, as to her staple manufacture, deprived of those resources; she was brought within a system of colonisation, but on worse terms than any of the plantations who were allowed to trade with each other.[384]

She could send her principal materials for manufacture to England only; but those manufactures were encouraged in England and discouraged in Ireland. The probable consequence of which was, and the event has answered the expectation, that we should take those manufactures from that country; and that, therefore, in those various trades which employ the greatest numbers of men, the English should work for our people; the rich should work for the poor.

Let the histories of both kingdoms, and the statute books of both parliaments be examined, and no precedent will be found for the Act of 1699, or for the system which it introduced.

The whole tenor of the English statutes relative to the trade of this country, and which, by our Act of the 10th of Henry VII., became a part of our commercial constitution, breathe a spirit totally repugnant to the principle of that law; and it is, therefore, with the utmost deference, submitted to those who have the power to decide whether this law was agreeable to the commercial constitution of Ireland, which, for 500 years, has never produced a similar instance.

It might be naturally supposed, by a person not versed in our story, that in the seventeenth century there had been some offence given or some demerit on our part. He would be surprised to hear that during this period our loyalty had been exemplary, and our sufferings on that account great. In 1641, great numbers of the Protestants of Ireland were destroyed, and many of them were deprived of their property and driven out of their country from their attachment to the English Government in this kingdom, and to that religion and constitution which they happily enjoyed under it. At the Revolution they were constant in the same principles, and successfully staked their lives and properties against domestic and foreign enemies in support of the rights of the English crown, and of the religious and civil liberties of Britain and of Ireland. They bravely shared with her in all her dangers, and liberally partook of all her adversities. Whatever were their rights, they had forfeited none of them. Whatever favours they enjoyed, they had new claims from their merit and their sufferings to a continuance of them. They now

---

[383] Sir William Petty mentions that "the English who have lands in Ireland were forced to trade only with strangers, and became unacquainted with their own country, and that England gained more than it lost by a free commerce (with Ireland), as exporting hither three times as much as it received from hence," and mentions his surprise at their being debarred from bringing commodities from America directly home, and being obliged to bring them round from England, with extreme hazard and loss.—"Political Survey of Ireland," p. 123.

[384] 22nd and 23rd Ch. II., ch. 26, sec. 11.

wanted more than ever the care of that fostering hand which, by rescuing them twice from oppression (obligations never to be forgotton by the Protestants of Ireland), established the liberties, confirmed the strength, and raised the glory of the British empire.

In speaking of a commercial system, it is not intended to touch upon the power of making or altering laws; the present subject leads us only to consider whether that power has been exercised in any instances contrary to reason, justice, and public utility.

When we consider, with the utmost deference to established authority, what is *reasonable, useful, and just*, principles equally applicable to an independent or a subordinate, to a rich or a poor country: *Quod æque pauperibus prodest, locupletibus æque.* Should any man talk of a conquest above 500 years since, between kingdoms long united like those, in blood, interest, and constitution, he does not speak to the purpose; he may as well talk of the conquest of the Norman, and use the antiquated language of obsolete despotism. I revere that conquest which has given to Ireland the common law and the Magna Charta of England.

When we consider what is *reasonable, useful, and just*, and address our sentiments to a nation renowned for wisdom and justice, should pride pervert the question, talk of the power of Britain, and, in the character of that great country, ask, like Tancred, who shall control me? I answer, like the sober Siffredi—*thyself*.

The power of regulating trade in a great empire is perverted, when exercised for the destruction of trade in any part of it; but whatever or wherever that power is, if it says to the subject on one side of a channel, you may work and navigate, buy and sell; and to the subject on the other side, you shall not work or navigate, buy or sell, but under such restrictions as will extinguish the genius and unnerve the arm of industry; I will only say that it uses a language repugnant to the free spirit of commerce, and of the British and Irish constitution.

Great eulogiums on the virtues of our people have been pronounced by some of the most respected English authors.[385] Yet indolence is objected to them by those who discourage their industry; but they do not reflect that each of these proceeds from habit, and that the noble observation made on virtue in general is equally applicable to industry; the day that it loses its liberty half of its vigour is gone.[386]

The great expenditure of money by England on account of this country is an argument more fit for the limited views of a compting-house than for the enlarged policy of statesmen deliberating on the general good of a great empire.

Very large sums, it is true, were advanced by England for the relief and recovery of Ireland; but these have been reimbursed fifty-fold by the profits and advantages which have since arisen to England from its trade and intercourse with this kingdom. This argument may be further pursued, but accounts of mutual benefits between intimate friends and near relations should always be kept open, and every attempt to strike a balance between them tends rather to raise jealousies than

[385] Sir John Davis and Sir Edward Cooke.
[386] Ἥμισυ γαρ τ' ἀρετῆς ἀποαίνυται δόυλιον ἦμαρ.

to promote good will.

It has been said that the interest of England required that those restraints should be imposed. The contrary has been shown; one of the maxims of her own law instructs us to enjoy our own property, so as not to injure that of our neighbour,[387] and the true interest of a great country lies in the population, wealth, and strength of the whole empire.

If this restrictive system was founded in justice and sound policy towards the middle and at the conclusion of the last century, the present state of the British empire requires new counsels and a system of commerce and of policy totally different from those which the circumstances of these countries, in the years 1663, 1670, and 1698, might have suggested.

But it is time to give your lordship a little relief before I enter into a new part of my subject.

I have the honour to be, My lord, &c.

---

[387] Sic utere tuo, alienum non lædas.

EIGHTH LETTER.

Dublin, 6th September, 1779.

My Lord,

Between the 23rd of October, 1641, and the same day in the year 1652, five hundred and four thousand of the inhabitants of Ireland are said to have perished and been wasted by the sword, plague, famine, hardship, and banishment.[388] If it had not been for the numbers of British which those wars had brought over,[389] and such who, either as adventurers or soldiers, seated themselves here on account of the satisfaction made to them in lands, the country had been, by the rebellion of 1641 and the plague that followed it, nearly desolate. At the restoration almost the whole property of the kingdom was in a state of the utmost anarchy and confusion. To satisfy the clashing interests of the numerous claimants, and to determine the various and intricate disputes that arose relative to titles, required a considerable length of time. Peace and settlement, or, to use the words of one of the Acts of Parliament[390] of that time, the repairing the ruins and desolation of the kingdom were the great objects of this period.

The English law[391] of 1663, restraining the exportation from Ireland to America, was at that time, and for some years after, scarcely felt in this kingdom, which had then little to export except live cattle, not proper for so distant a market.

The Act of Settlement, passed in Ireland the year before this restrictive law, and the explanatory statute for the settlement of this kingdom, was not enacted until two years after. The country continued for a considerable time in a state of litigation, which is never favourable to industry. In 1661, the people must have been poor; the number of them of all degrees who paid poll money in that year was about 360,000.[392] In 1672, when the country had greatly improved, the manufacture bestowed upon a year's exportation from Ireland did not exceed eight thousand pounds,[393] and the clothing trade had not then arrived to what it had been before the last rebellion. But still the kingdom had much increased in wealth, though not in manufactured exports. The customs which set in 1656 for £12,000 yearly were, in 1672, worth £80,000[394] yearly, and the improvement in domestic wealth, that is to say, in building, planting, furniture, coaches, &c., is said to have

[388] Sir William Petty's "Political Survey of Ireland," p. 19.
[389] Sir William Temple, vol. iii., p. 7.
[390] The Act of Explanation.
[391] 15 Ch. II.
[392] Sir W. Petty, p. 9.
[393] Ib. pp. 9 and 110.
[394] Sir W. Petty, p. 89.

advanced from 1652 to 1673 in a proportion of from one to four. Sir William Petty, in the year 1672, complains not of the restraints on the exportation from Ireland to America,[395] but of the prohibition of exporting our cattle to England, and of our being obliged to unlade in that kingdom[396] the ships bound from America to Ireland, the latter regulation he considers as highly prejudicial to this country.[397]

The immediate object of Ireland at this time seems to have been to get materials to employ her people at home, without thinking of foreign exportations. When we advanced in the export of our woollen goods the law of 1663,[398] which excluded them from the American markets, must have been a great loss to this kingdom; and after we were allowed to export our linens to the British colonies in America, the restraints imposed by the law of 1670 upon our importations from thence became more prejudicial, and will be much more so if ever the late extension of our exports to America should under those restraints have any effect. For it is certainly a great discouragement to the carrying on trade with any country where we are allowed only to sell our manufactures and produce, but are not permitted to carry from them directly to our own country their principal manufactures or produce. The people to whom we are thus permitted to sell want the principal inducement for dealing with us, and the great spring of commerce, which is mutual exchange, is wanting between us.

As the British legislature has thought it reasonable to extend, to a very considerable degree, our exportation to their colonies, and has, doubtless, intended that this favour should be useful to Ireland, it is hoped that those restraints on the importation from thence, which must render that favour of little effect, will be no longer continued.

From those considerations it is evident that many strong reasons respecting Ireland are now to be found against the continuance of those restrictive laws of 1663 and 1670, that did not exist at the time of making them.

The prohibition of 1699 was immediately and universally felt in this country; but in the course of human events various and powerful reasons have arisen against the continuance of that statute, which did not exist, and could not have been foreseen when it was enacted.

At the Restoration the inhabitants of Ireland consisted of three different nations—English, Scotch, and Irish—divided by political and religious principles, exasperated against each other by former animosities, and by present contests for property. When the settlement of the country was completed, the people became industrious, manufactures greatly increased, and the kingdom began to flourish. The prohibition of exporting cattle to England, and perhaps that of importing directly from America the materials of other manufactures, obliged the Irish to increase and to manufacture their own material. They made so great a progress in both, from 1672 to 1687, that in the latter year the exports of the woollen manufacture alone amounted in value to £70,521 14s. 0d.

[395] Ib., pp. 9 and 10.
[396] Ib, pp. 34, 71, 125.
[397] Ib, pp. 34, 71, 125.
[398] 15 Ch. II., ch. 7.

But the religious and civil animosities continued. The papists objected to the settlement of property made after the Restoration,[399] wished to reverse the outlawries, and to rescind the laws on which that settlement was founded, hoped to establish their own as the national religion, to get the power of the kingdom into their own hands, and to effect all those purposes by a king of their own religion. They endeavoured to attain all those objects by laws[400] passed at a meeting which they called a parliament, held under this prince after his abdication; and by their conduct at this period, as well as in the year 1642,[401] showed dispositions unfavourable to the subordination of Ireland to the Crown of England. They could not be supposed to be well affected to that great prince who defeated all their purposes.

At the time of the revolution the numbers of our people were again very much reduced; but a great majority of the remaining inhabitants consisted of papists. Those, notwithstanding their disappointment at that era, were thought to entertain expectations of the restoration of their Popish king, and designs unfavourable to the established constitution in Church and State. It is not to the present purpose to inquire how long this disposition prevailed. It cannot be doubted but that this was the opinion conceived of their views and principles at the time of passing this law in the year 1699.

England could not then consider a country under such unfortunate circumstances as any great additional strength to it. Foreign Protestants were invited to settle in it, and the emigration of papists in great numbers to other countries was allowed, if not encouraged. Though at this period a regard to liberty as well as to economy, occasioned the disbanding of all the army in England, except 7,000, it was thought necessary for the security of Ireland that an army of 12,000 men should be kept there; and for many years afterwards it was not allowed that this army should be recruited in this kingdom. This distinction of parties in Ireland was in those times the mainspring in every movement relative to that kingdom, and affected not only political but commercial regulations. The reason assigned by the English statute, allowing the exportation of Irish linen cloth to the plantations, is, after reciting the restrictive law of 1663,[402] "*yet*, forasmuch as the Protestant interest of Ireland ought to be supported, by giving the utmost encouragement to the linen manufactures of that kingdom, in tender regard to her Majesty's good Protestant subjects of her said kingdom, be it enacted," &c.

The papists, then disabled from acquiring permanent property in lands, had not the same interest with Protestants in the defence of their country and in the prosperity of the British Empire. But those seeds of disunion and diffidence no

[399] Carte, vol. ii., pp. 425 to 428, 465.

[400] Archb. Bishop King's State, 209. James II., in his speech from the throne in Ireland, recommended the repeal of the Act of Settlement.

[401] Their demands in 1642 were the restitution of all the plantation lands to the old inhabitants, repeal of Poyning's Act, &c.—Macaulay's Hist., vol. iii, p. 222. In the meeting called a parliament, held by James in Ireland, they repealed the Acts of Settlement and Explanation, passed a law that the Parliament of England cannot bind Ireland, and against writs of error and appeal to England.

[402] 3rd and 4th Anne, ch. 8.

longer remain. No man looks now for the return of the exiled family any more than for that of Perken Warbec; and the repeal of Magna Charta is as much expected as of the Act of Settlement. The papists, indulged with the exercise of their religious worship, and now at liberty to acquire permanent property in lands, are interested as well as Protestants in the security and prosperity of this country; and sensible of the benign influence of our Sovereign, and of the protection and happiness which they enjoy under his reign, seem to be as well affected to the King and to the constitution of the State as any other class of subjects, and at this most dangerous crisis have contributed their money to raise men for his Majesty's service, and declared their readiness, had the laws permitted, to have taken arms for the defence of their country. They owe much to the favour and protection of the Crown, and to the liberal and benevolent spirit of the British legislature which led the way to their relief, and they are peculiarly interested to cultivate the good opinion of their Sovereign, and of their fellow-subjects in Great Britain.

The numbers of our people, since the year 1698, are more than doubled; but in point of real strength to the British Empire are increased in a proportion of above eight to one. In the year 1698 the numbers of our people did not much, if at all, exceed one million. Of these 300,000 are thought to be a liberal allowance for Protestants of all denominations. It is now supposed that there are not less in this kingdom than 2,500,000 loyal and affectionate subjects to his Majesty, and well affected to the constitution and happiness of their country.

A political and commercial constitution, if it could have been considered as wisely framed for the years 1663, 1670, and 1698, ought to be reconsidered in the year 1779; what might have been good and necessary policy in the government of one million of men disunited among themselves, and a majority of them not to be relied upon in support of their king and of the laws and constitution of their country, is bad policy in the government of two millions and a-half of men now united among themselves, and all interested in the support of the Crown, the laws, and the constitution.

What might have been sufficient employment, and the means of acquiring a competent subsistence for one million of people, when a man, by working two days in the week, might have earned a sufficient support for him and his family, will never answer for two millions and a-half of people,[403] when the hard labour of six days in the week can scarcely supply a scanty subsistence. Nor can the resources which enabled us in the last century to remit £200,000 yearly to England[404] support remittances to the amount of more than six times that sum.

Let the reasons for this restrictive system at the time of its formation be examined, and let us judge impartially whether any one of the purposes then intended has been answered. The reasons respecting America were to confine the Plantation trade to England, and to make that country a storehouse of all commodities for its colonies. But the commercial jealousy that has prevailed among the different states of Europe has made it difficult for any nation to keep great markets to herself in exclusion of the rest of the world. It was not foreseen at those periods that the col-

[403] Sir W. Petty's "Survey."
[404] Ib., p. 117.

onies, whilst they all continued dependent, should have traded with foreign nations, notwithstanding the utmost efforts of Great Britain to prevent it. It was not foreseen that those colonies would have refused to have taken any commodities whatever from their parent country, that they should afterwards have separated themselves from her empire, declared themselves independent, resisted her fleets and armies, obtained the most powerful alliances, and occasioned the most dangerous and destructive war in which Great Britain was ever engaged. Nor could it have been foreseen that Ireland, excluded from almost all direct intercourse with them, should have been nearly undone by the contest. The reasons then respecting America no longer exist, and whatever may be the event of the conflict, will never exist to the extent expected when this system of restraints and penalties was adopted.

The reasons relating to Ireland have failed also. The circumstances of this country relative to the woollen manufacture are totally changed since the year 1699. The Lords and Commons of England appear to have founded the law of that year on the proportion which they supposed that the charge of the woollen manufacture in England then bore to the charge of that manufacture in Ireland. In the representation from the Commissioners of Trade, laid before both houses,[405] they think it a reasonable conjecture to take the difference between both wool and labour in the two countries to be one-third; and estimating on that supposition, they find that 43⅞ per cent. may be laid on broadcloth exported out of Ireland, more than on the like cloth exported out of England, to bring them both to an equality. This must have been an alarming representation to England.

But if those calculations were just at the time, which is very doubtful, the supposed facts on which they were founded do certainly no longer exist. Wool is now generally at a higher price in Ireland than in England, and the trifling difference in the price of labour is more than overbalanced by this and the other circumstances in favour of England, which have been before stated; and that those facts supposed in 1698, and the inferences drawn from them, have no foundation in the present state of this country is plain from the experience every day, which shows that instead of our underselling the English, they undersell us in our own markets.

Besides our exclusion from foreign markets, England had two objects in the discouragement of our woollen trade.

It was intended that Ireland should send her wool to England, and take from that country her woollen manufactures.[406] It has been already shown that the first object has not been attained, the second has been carried so far as, for the future, to defeat its own purpose. Whilst our own manufacturers were starving for want of

---

[405] Order 14th March, 1698, Lords' Journ., vol. xvi. Eng. Com. Journs., 18th Jan., 1698, vol. xii., p. 440.

[406] The Commissioners of Trade, in their representation dated 11th November, 1697, relating to the trade between England and Ireland, advise a duty to be laid upon the importation of oil, upon teasles, whether imported or *growing* there, and upon *all the utensils* employed in the making any woollen manufactures, on the utensils of worsted combers, and particularly a duty by the yard upon all cloth and woollen stuffs, except friezes, before they are taken off the loom. Eng. Com. Journ., vol. x., p. 428.

employment, and our wool sold for less than one-half its usual price, we have imported from England, in the years 1777 and 1778, woollen goods to the enormous amount of £715,740 13s. 0d., as valued at our Custom House, and of the manufactures of linen, cotton, and silk mixed, to the amount of £98,086 1s. 11d., making in the whole in those two years of distress, £813,826 14s. 11d.[407] Between 20 and 30,000 of our manufacturers in those branches were in those two years supported by public charity. From this fact it is hoped that every reasonable man will allow the necessity of our using our own manufactures. Agreements among our people for this purpose are not, as it has been supposed, a new idea in this country. It was never so universal as at present, but has been frequently resorted to in times of distress. In the sessions of 1703, 1705, and 1707,[408] the House of Commons resolved unanimously, that it would greatly conduce to the relief of the poor and the good of the kingdom, that the inhabitants thereof should use none other but the manufactures of this kingdom in their apparel and the furniture of their houses; and in the last of those sessions the members engaged their honours to each other, that they would conform to the said resolution. The not importing goods from England is one of the remedies recommended by the council of trade in 1676, for alleviating some distress that was felt at that time;[409] and Sir William Temple, a zealous friend to the trade and manufactures of England, recommends to Lord Essex, then Lord Lieutenant, "to introduce, as far as can be, a vein of parsimony throughout the country in all things that are not perfectly the native growths and manufactures."[410]

The people of England cannot reasonably object to a conduct of which they have given a memorable example.[411] In 1697 the English House of Lords presented an address to King William to discourage the use and wearing of all sorts of furniture and cloths, not of the growth or manufacture of that kingdom; and beseech him by his royal example effectually to encourage the use and wearing of all sorts of furniture and wearing cloths that are the growth of that kingdom, or manufactured there; and King William assures them that he would give the example to his subjects,[412] and would endeavour to make it effectually followed. The reason assigned by the Lords for this address was that the trade of the nation had suffered by the late long and expensive war. But it does not appear that there was any pressing necessity at the time, or that their manufacturers were starving for want of employment.

Common sense must discover to every man that, where foreign trade is restrained, discouraged, or prevented in any country, and where that country has the materials of manufactures, a fruitful soil, and numerous inhabitants, the home-trade is its best resource. If this is thought, by men of great knowledge, to be the

---

[407] See in the Appendix an account of those articles imported from England into Ireland for ten years, commencing in 1769, and ending in 1778.

[408] Com. Journ., vol. iii., pp. 348, 548.

[409] Sir W. Petty's "Political Survey," p. 123.

[410] Sir W. Temple, vol. iii., p. 11.

[411] Lord's Journ., 16th Feb., 1697.

[412] Lord's Journ., 19th Feb., 1697.

most valuable of all trades,[413] because it makes the speediest and the surest returns, and because it increases at the same time two capitals in the same country, there is no nation on the globe whose wealth, population, strength, and happiness would be promoted by such a trade in a greater degree than ours.[414]

Two other reasons were assigned for this prohibition: that the Irish had shown themselves unwilling to promote the linen manufacture,[415] and that there were great quantities of wool in Ireland. But they have since cultivated the linen trade with great success, and great numbers of their people are employed in it. Of late years by the operation of the land-carriage bounty, agriculture has increased in a degree never before known in this country; extensive tracts of lands, formerly sheep-pasture, are now under tillage, and much greater rents are given for that purpose than can be paid by stocking with sheep; the quantity of wool is greatly diminished from what it was in the year 1699, supposing it to have been then equal to the quantity in 1687,[416] it has been for several years lessening, and is not likely to be increased. In those two important circumstances the grounds of the apprehensions of England have ceased, and the state of Ireland has been materially altered since the year 1699.

Another reason respecting England and foreign States, particularly France, has failed. England was, in 1698, in possession of the woollen trade in most of the foreign markets, and expected still to continue to supply them, as appears by the preamble of her Statute passed in that year.

She at that time expected to keep this manufacture to herself. The people of Leeds, Halifax, and Newberry,[417] petition the House of Commons "that by some means the woollen manufacture may be prevented from being set up in foreign countries;" and the Commons, in their address, mention the keeping it as much as possible *entire* to themselves. But experience has proved the vanity of those expectations; several other countries cultivate this trade with success. France now undersells her. England has lost some of those markets, and it is thought probable that Ireland, if admitted to them, might have preserved and may now recover the trade that England has lost.

A perseverance in this restrictive policy will be ruinous to the trade of Great Britain. Whatever may be the state of America, great numbers of the inhabitants of Ireland, if the circumstances of this country shall continue to be the same as at present in respect of trade, will emigrate there; this will give strength to that part of the empire on which Great Britain can least, and take it from that part on which at present she may most securely depend. But this is not all the mischief; those

[413] See Dr. Smith's "Wealth of Nations."

[414] The consumption of our own people is the best and greatest market for the product and manufactures of our own country. Foreign trade is but a part of the benefit arising from the woollen manufacture, and the least part; it is a small article in respect to the benefit arising to the community, and Dr. Smith affirms that all the foreign markets of England cannot be equal to one-twentieth part of her own.—Dr. Smith's "Memoirs of Wool," vol. ii., pp. 113, 529, 530, and 556, from the *British Merchant* and Dr. Davenant.

[415] Address of Eng. Commons, *ante.*

[416] King's Stat., pp. 160, 161.

[417] Eng. Com. Journ., vol. xii., pp. 514, 523, 528.

emigrants will be mostly manufacturers, and will transfer to America the woollen and linen manufactures, to the great prejudice of those trades in England, Scotland, and Ireland; and then one of the means used to keep the colonies dependent by introducing this country into a system of colonisation, will be the occasion of lessening, if not dissolving, the connection between them and their parent State.

Great Britain, weakened in her extremities, should fortify the heart of her empire; Great Britain, with powerful foreign enemies united in lasting bonds against her, and with scarcely any foreign alliance to sustain her, should exert every possible effort to strengthen herself at home. The number of people in Ireland have more than doubled in fourscore years. How much more rapid would be the increase if the growth of the human race was cherished by finding sufficient employment and food for this prolific nation! it would probably double again in half a century. What a vast accession of strength such numbers of brave and active men, living almost within the sound of a trumpet, must bring to Great Britain, now said to be decreasing considerably in population!—a greater certainty than double those numbers dispersed in distant parts of the globe, the expense of defending and governing of which must at all times be great. Sir W. Temple,[418] in 1673, takes notice of the circumstances prejudicial to the trade and riches of Ireland, which had hitherto, he says, made it of more loss than value to England. They have already been mentioned. The course of time has removed some of them, and the wisdom and philanthropy of Britain may remove the rest. "Without these circumstances (says that honest and able statesman), the native fertility of the soils and seas, in so many rich commodities, improved by multitudes of people and industry, with the advantage of so many excellent havens, and a situation so commodious for all sorts of foreign trade, must needs have rendered this kingdom one of the richest in Europe, and made a mighty increase both of strength and revenue to the crown of England."[419]

During this century, Ireland has been, without exaggeration, a mine of wealth to England, far beyond what any calculation has yet made it. When poor and thinly inhabited she was an expense and a burden to England; when she had acquired some proportion of riches and grew more numerous, she was one of the principal sources of her wealth. When she becomes poor again, those advantages are greatly diminished. The exports from Great Britain to Ireland, in 1778,[420] were less than the medium value of the four preceding years in a sum of £634,444 3s. 0d; and in the year 1779, Great Britain is obliged, partly at her own expense, to defend this country, and for that purpose has generously bestowed out of her own exchequer a large sum of money. Those facts demonstrate that the poverty of Ireland ever has been a drain, and her riches an influx of wealth to England, to which the greater part of it will ever flow, and it imports not to that country through what channel; but the source must be cleared from obstructions, or the stream cannot continue to flow.

---

[418] Vol. iii., p. 8.

[419] See Sir John Davis's "Discourses," pp. 5, 6, 194.

[420] Summary of Imports and Exports to and from Ireland, laid before the British House of Commons in 1779.

Such a liberal system would increase the wealth of this kingdom by means that would strengthen the hands of government, and promote the happiness of the people. Ireland would be then able to contribute largely to the support of the British Empire, not only from the increase of her wealth, but from the more equal distribution of it into a greater number of hands among the various orders of the community. The present inability of Ireland arises principally from this circumstance, that her lower and middle classes have little or no property, and are not able, to any considerable amount, either to pay taxes or consume those commodities that are the usual subjects of them; and this has been the consequence of the laws which prevent trade and discourage manufactures. The same quantity of property distributed through the different classes of the people would supply resources much superior to those which can be found in the present state of Ireland.[421] The increase of people there under its present restraints makes but a small addition to the resources of the State in respect of taxes.[422] In 1685, the amount of the inland excise in Ireland was £75,169. In 1762, it increased only to £92,842. Those years are taken as periods of a considerable degree of prosperity in Ireland. The people had increased, from 1685 to 1762, in a proportion of nearly 7 to 4,[423] which appears from this circumstance, that in 1685 hearth-money amounted to £32,659, and in 1762 to £56,611. At the former period the law made to restrain and discourage the principal trade and manufacture of Ireland had not been made. There were then vast numbers of sheep in Ireland, and the woollen manufacture was probably in a flourishing state. At the former of those periods the lower classes of the people were able to consume excisable commodities; in the latter they lived for the most part on the immediate produce of the soil. The numbers of people in a state, like those of a private family, if the individuals have the means of acquiring, add to the wealth, and if they have not those means, to the poverty of the community. Population is not always a proof of the prosperity of a nation; the people may be very numerous and very poor and wretched. A temperate climate, fruitful soil, bays and rivers well stocked with fish, the habits of life among the lower classes, and a long peace, are sufficient to increase the numbers of people: these are the true wealth of every state that has wisdom to encourage the industry of its inhabitants, and a country which supplies in abundance the materials for that industry. If the state or the family should discourage industry, and not allow one of the family to work, because another is of the same trade, the consequences to the great or the

---

[421] Those states are least able to pay great charges for public disbursements whose wealth resteth chiefly in the hands of the nobility and gentry.—Bac., vol. i., p. 10; Smith's "Wealth of Nations," vol. ii., p. 22.

[422] A very judicious friend of mine has, with great pains and attention, made a calculation of the numbers of people in Ireland in the year 1774, and he makes the numbers of people to amount to 2,325,041; but supposes his calculation to be under the real number. I have, therefore, followed the calculation commonly received, which makes their number amount to 2,500,000. He computes, as has been before mentioned, the persons who reside in houses of one hearth, to be 1,877,220. Those find it very difficult to pay hearth money, and are thought to be unable to pay any other taxes. If this is so, according to this calculation, there are but 447,821 people in Ireland able to pay taxes.

[423] Ireland was much more numerous in 1685 than at any time, after the Revolution, during that century, there having been a great waste of people in the rebellion at that era.

little community must be equally fatal.

Is there not business enough in this great world for the people of two adjoining islands, without depressing the inhabitants of one of them? Let the magnanimity and philanthropy of Great Britain address her poor sister kingdom in the same language which the good-natured Uncle Toby uses to the fly in setting it at liberty:—"Poor fly; there's room enough for thee and me."

I have the honour to be, My Lord, &c.

NINTH LETTER.

Dublin, 10th Sept., 1779.

MY LORD,

Besides those already mentioned, various other commercial restraints and prohibitions give the British trader and manufacturer many great and important advantages over the Irish. Whilst our markets are at all times open to all their productions and manufactures, with inconsiderable duties on the import, their markets are open or shut against us as suits their conveniency. On several articles of the first importance, and on almost all our own manufactures imported into Great Britain, duties are imposed equal to a prohibition. In the instance of woollen goods, theirs in our ports pay but a small duty; ours in their ports are loaded with duties[424] which amount to a prohibition.[425] Theirs on the exportation are subject to no duty; ours, if permitted to be exported, would, as the law now stands, be subject to a duty[426] over and above that payable for alnage and for the alnager's fee. If the Act of 1699 was repealed, the English would still have many great advantages over us in the woollen trade.

In our staple manufacture, the bounties given on the exportation of white and brown Irish linen from Great Britain would still continue that trade in the hands of the British merchant. On all coloured linens a duty[427] equal to a prohibition is imposed on the importation into Great Britain; but theirs, imported to us, are subject[428] to ten per cent., and under that duty they have imported considerably. This inequality of duty, and the bounty given by the British Act of the tenth of Geo. III., on the exportation of their chequered and striped linens from Great Britain, secures to them the continuance of the great superiority which they have acquired over us in those very valuable branches of this trade. In many other articles they have given themselves great advantages. Beer they export to us in such quantities as almost to ruin our brewery; but they prevent our exportation to them by

---

[424] 12 Ch. II., ch. 4. Eng.

[425] Yet, in favour of Great Britain, old and new drapery imported into Ireland from other countries are subject to duties equal to a prohibition. Ir. Act 14th and 15th, Ch. II., ch. 8.

[426] On every piece of old drapery exported, containing thirty-six yards, and so for a greater or lesser quantity, 3s. 4d., and of new drapery 9d., for the subsidy of alnage and alnager's fee. See 17th and 18th Ch. II., ch. 15. Ir. But the English have taken off these and all other duties from their manufactures made or mixed with wool. Eng. Act 11 and 12 W. III., ch. 20.

[427] 30 per cent. by the British acts of 9 and 10 Anne, ch. 39., and 12 Anne, ch. 9.

[428] This tax is *ad valorem*, and the linen not valued.

duties, laid on the import there, equal to a prohibition. Of malt they make large exports to us, to the prejudice of our agriculture, but have absolutely prohibited our exportation of that commodity to them. Some manufactures they retain solely to themselves, which we are prohibited from exporting, and cannot import from any country but Great Britain, as glass of all kinds. Hops they do not allow us to import from any other place, and in a facetious style of interdiction, pronounce such importation to be a common nuisance.[429] They go further, and by laying a duty on the export, and denying the draw-back, oblige the Irish consumer to pay a tax appropriated, it is said, to the payment of a British debt. I shall make no political, but the subject requires a commercial observation—it is this: the man who keeps a market solely to himself, in exclusion of all others, whether he appears as buyer[430] or seller, fixes his own price, and becomes the arbiter of the profit and loss of every customer.

The various manufactures[431] made or mixed with cotton are subject, by several British Acts, to duties on the importation amounting to 25 per cent.

By another Act, penalties[432] are imposed on wearing any of those manufactures in Great Britain, unless made in that country. Those laws have effectually excluded the Irish manufactures, in all those branches, from the British markets; and it has been already shown that they cannot be sent to the American. From Great Britain into Ireland all those articles are imported in immense quantities, being subject here to duties amounting to 10 per cent. only.

But it would be tedious to descend into a further detail, and disgusting to write a book of rates instead of a letter.[433]

Their superior capitals and expertness give them decisive advantages in every species of trade and manufacture. By the extension of the commerce of Ireland, Great Britain would acquire new and important advantages, not only by the wealth it would bring to that country, and the increase of strength to the empire, but by opening to the British merchant new sources of trade from Ireland.

It is time to draw to a conclusion. I have reviewed my letters to your lordship, for the purpose of avoiding every possible occasion of offence. I flatter myself every reader will discern that they have been written with upright and friendly intentions, not to excite jealousies, but to remove prejudices, to moderate, and conciliate; and that they are intended as an appeal, not to the passions of the multitude, but to the wisdom, justice, and generosity of Britain. Shakespeare could place a tongue in every wound of Cæsar; but Antony meant to inflame; and the only purpose of those letters is to persuade. I have, therefore, not even removed the mantle except where necessity required it.

---

[429] Brit. Act, 9 Anne, ch. 12.

[430] Hence it is that the price of wool in England is said to be 50 per cent. below the market price of Europe.—Smith's "Memoir's of Wool."

[431] 12 Ch. II., ch. 5. 3 and 4 Anne, ch. 4. 4 and 5 W. and M., ch. 5.

[432] 7 G. I., ch. 7.

[433] When the commercial restraints of Ireland are the subject, a source of occasional and ruinous restrictions ought not to be passed over. Since the year 1740, there have been twenty-four embargoes in Ireland, one of which lasted three years.

In extraordinary cases where the facts are stronger than the voice of the pleader, it is not unusual to allow the client to speak for himself. Will you, my lord, one of the leading advocates for Ireland, allow her to address her elder sister, and to state her own case; not in the strains of passion or resentment, nor in the tone of remonstrance, but with a modest enumeration of unexaggerated facts in pathetic simplicity. She will tell her, with a countenance full of affection and tenderness, "I have received from you invaluable gifts—the law of[434] common right, your great charter, and the fundamentals of your constitution. The temple of liberty in your country has been frequently fortified, improved, and embellished; mine, erected many centuries since the perfect model of your own, you will not suffer me to strengthen, secure, or repair; firm and well-cemented as it is, it must moulder under the hand of Time for want of that attention which is due to the venerable fabric.[435] We are connected by the strongest ties of natural affection, common security, and a long interchange of the kindest offices on both sides. But for more than a century you have, in some instances, mistaken our mutual interest. I sent you my herds and my flocks, filled your people with abundance, and gave them leisure to attend to more profitable pursuits than the humble employment of shepherds and of herdsmen. But you rejected my produce,[436] and reprobated this intercourse in terms the most opprobrious. I submitted; the temporary loss was mine, but the perpetual prejudice your own. I incited my children to industry, and gave them my principal materials to manufacture. Their honest labours were attended with moderate success, but sufficient to awaken the commercial jealousy of some of your sons; indulging their groundless apprehensions, you desired my materials, and discouraged the industry of my people. I complied with your wishes, and gave to your children the bread of my own; but the enemies of our race were the gainers. They applied themselves with tenfold increase to those pursuits which were restrained in my people, who would have added to the wealth and strength of your empire what, by this fatal error, you transferred to foreign nations. You held out another object to me with promises of the utmost encouragement. I wanted the means, but I obtained them from other countries, and have long cultivated, at great expense, and with the most unremitted efforts, that species of industry which you recommended. You soon united with another great family, engaged in the same pursuit, which you were also obliged to encourage among them, and afterwards embarked in it yourself, and became my rival in that which you had destined for my principal support. This support is now become inadequate to the increased number of my offspring, many of whom want the means of subsistence. My ports are ever hospitably open for your reception, and shut, whenever your interest requires it, against all others; but yours are, in many instances, barred against me. With your dominions in Asia, Africa, and America my sons were long deprived of all beneficial intercourse, and yet to those colonies I transported my treasures for the payment of your armies, and in a war waged for their defence

[434] The common law of England.

[435] Heads of bills for passing into a law the Habeas Corpus Act, and that for making the tenure of judges during good behaviour, have repeatedly passed the Irish House of Commons, but were not returned.

[436] The Eng. Act of Ch. II, ch. —, calls the importation of cattle from Ireland a common nuisance.

one hundred thousand of my sons fought by your side.[437] Conquest attended our arms. You gained a great increase of empire and of commerce, and my people a further extension of restraints and prohibitions.[438] In those efforts I have exhausted my strength, mortgaged my territories, and am now sinking under the pressure of enormous debts, contracted from my zealous attachment to your interests, to the extension of your empire, and the increase of your glory. By the present unhappy war for the recovery of those colonies, from which they were long excluded, my children are reduced to the lowest ebb of poverty and distress. It is true you have lately, with the kindest intentions, allowed me an extensive liberty of selling to the inhabitants of those parts of your empire; but they have no inducement to buy, because I cannot take their produce in return. Your liberality has opened a new fountain, but your caution will not suffer me to draw from it. The stream of commerce intended to refresh the exhausted strength of my children flies untasted from their parched lips.

"The common parent of all has been equally beneficent to us both. We both possess in great abundance the means of industry and happiness. My fields are not less fertile nor my harbours less numerous than yours. My sons are not less renowned than your own for valour, justice, and generosity. Many of them are your descendants, and have some of your best blood in their veins. But the narrow policy of man has counteracted the instincts and the bounties of nature. In the midst of those fertile fields some of my children perish before my eyes for want of food, and others fly for refuge to hostile nations.

Suffer no longer, respected sister, the narrow jealousy of commerce to mislead the wisdom and to impair the strength of your state. Increase my resources, they shall be yours, my riches and strength, my poverty and weakness will become your own. What a triumph to our enemies, and what an affliction to me, in the present distracted circumstances of the empire, to see my people reduced by the necessity of avoiding famine, to the resolution of trafficing almost solely with themselves! Great and powerful enemies are combined against you; many of your distant connections have deserted you. Increase your strength at home, open and extend the numerous resources of my country, of which you have not hitherto availed yourself, or allowed me the benefit. Our increased force, and the full exertions of our strength, will be the most effectual means of resisting the combination formed against you by foreign enemies and distant subjects, and of giving new lustre to our crowns, and happiness and contentment to our people."

---

[437] This number of Irishmen was computed to have served in the fleets and armies of Great Britain during the last war.

[438] The furs of Canada, the indigo of Florida, the sugars of Dominica, St. Vincent, and the Grenadas, with every other valuable production of those acquisitions Ireland was prohibited to receive but through another channel. Her poverty scarcely gathered a crumb from the sumptuous table of her sister.

APPENDIX.

APPENDIX.—NO. I.

Quantity of Wool, Woollen, and Worsted Yarn exported from Ireland to Great Britain in the following years:—

Years Ending the 25th of March.	WOOL.		YARN.			
			Woollen.		Worsted.	
	stones.	lbs.	stones.	lbs.	stones.	lbs.
1764	10,128	6	9,991	14	139,412	12
1795	17,316	0	13,450	12	149,915	9
1766	21,722	13	7,980	0	152,122	0
1767	48,733	8	7,553	0	151,940	9
1768	28,521	11	11,387	6	157,721	3
1769	3,840	16	5,012	0	131,365	2
1770	2,578	0	3,833	0	117,735	9
1771	2,118	5	4,868	2	139,378	14
1772	2,045	6	5,947	0	115,904	4
1773	1,839	2	—		94,098	10
1774	1,007	11	—		63,920	10
1775	2,007	13	—		78,896	14
1776	1,059	15	—		86,527	0
1777	1,734	7	—		114,703	2
1778	1,665	12	—		122,755	15

APPENDIX.—NO. II.

Years Ending the 25th of March.	DRAPERY.								LINEN COTTON.		
	New.				Old.				Silk, mixed manufacture.		
	Quantity.	Value.			Quantity.	Value.			Value.		
		£	s.	d.		£	s.	d.	£	s.	d.
1769	394,553	49,319	3	9	207,117	144,982	8	6	13,402	10	7
1770	462,499	57,812	7	6	249,666	174,766	14	6	20,907	18	2½
1771	362,096	45,262	0	0	217,395	152,176	10	0	20,282	5	8
1772	314,703	39,337	18	9	153,566	107,496	4	0	14,081	15	6½
1773	387,143	48,392	17	6	200,065	147,045	13	6	20,472	7	3½
1774	461,407	57,675	17	6	282,317	197,621	18	0	21,611	10	3¼
1775	465,611	58,201	9	4½	281,379	196,965	13	0	24,234	16	9½
1776	676,485	84,560	12	6	290,215	203,150	10	0	30,371	16	8½
1777	731,819	91,477	8	9	381,330	266,931	0	0	45,411	3	7
1778	741,426	92,678	6	3	378,077	264,653	18	0	52,675	1	11

APPENDIX.—NO. III.

An account of the Quantity of Linen Cloth exported out of Ireland to Great Britain and Plantations, prior to the year 1743.

Years Ending the 25th of March.	Linen Cloth exported to	
	Great Britain.	Plantations.
	Yards.	Yards.
1705	739,278	19,742
1706	1,325,771	62,727
1707	1,847,564	81,037
1708	343,359	29,606
1709	1,539,250	113,939
1710	1,528,185	136,844
1711	1,131,629	89,262
1712	1,320,968	43,011
1713	1,721,003	86,357
1714	2,071,814	91,916
1715	2,000,581	133,752
1716	1,968,568	195,825

1717	2,260,243	151,240
1718	2,120,075	113,790
1719	2,235,357	117,288
1720	2,560,113	69,579
1721	2,398,103	95,488
1722	3,036,431	127,934
1723	4,060,402	112,952
1724	3,767,063	94,816
1725	3,755,430	70,052
1726	4,231,676	117,213
1727	4,596,089	151,977
1728	4,517,152	140,049
1729	3,701,485	183,363
1730	3,821,188	218,220
1731	3,591,316	137,039
1733	4,621,127	129,244
1734	5,194,241	213,250
1735	6,508,748	202,759
1736	6,168,333	262,242
1737	5,758,408	309,827
1738	4,897,169	232,947
1739	5,737,834	197,671
1740	6,403,569	183,471
1741	6,760,025	394,374
1742	6,793,009	244,546

POSTSCRIPT.

Since these papers were sent to the press, the Commons of Ireland have, in their address to his Majesty, resolved, unanimously, "that it is not by temporary expedients, but by a free trade alone that this nation is now to be saved from impending ruin." And the Lords have in their address unanimously entered into a resolution of the same import.

INDEX.

U

Usher In Buck's School *Li*

V

Voted For The Union *Xlviii*

W

Walker's Hibernian Magazine *Xxvii*
Wealth Of Nations *31, 32, 35, 61, 63*
Wellington Correspondence *Lii*
Wesley *Xxix*
White Boys *Lxvi, 20*
Will *Xliv, Xlv, 67*
Winstanley's Poems *Xv*
Wool Trade *Xi, Lxi, Lxii, Lxiv, Lxvii, Lxviii*

Y

Yelverton *Xii, Xxx, Xxxii, Xl, Xlii, Xliii*

Lector House believes that a society develops through a two-fold approach of continuous learning and adaptation, which is derived from the study of classic literary works spread across the historic timeline of literature records. Therefore, we aim at reviving, repairing and redeveloping all those inaccessible or damaged but historically as well as culturally important literature across subjects so that the future generations may have an opportunity to study and learn from past works to embark upon a journey of creating a better future.

This book is a result of an effort made by Lector House towards making a contribution to the preservation and repair of original ancient works which might hold historical significance to the approach of continuous learning across subjects.

HAPPY READING & LEARNING!

LECTOR HOUSE LLP
E-MAIL: lectorpublishing@gmail.com